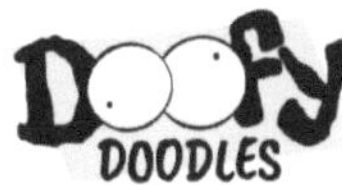

DRAW 25 MONSTERS

BADLY!

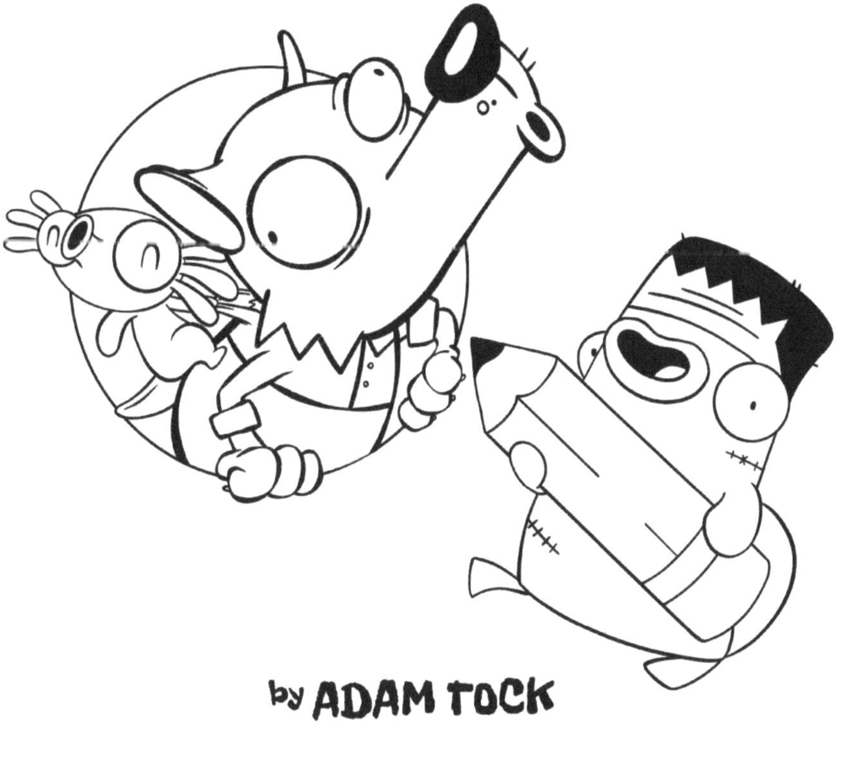

by **ADAM TOCK**

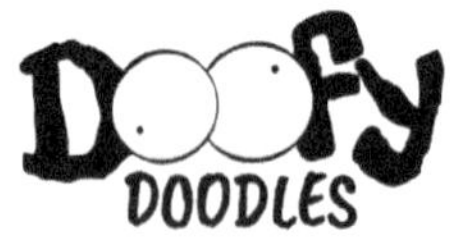

Obscure & Company LLC
1839 Winnetka Ave.
Northfield, IL 60093
https://www.obscureandco.com

ISBN: 979-8-9857620-5-1

Printed in the United States of America
First Edition

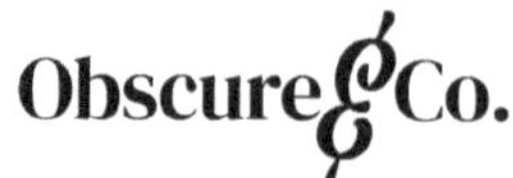

TABLE OF CONTENTS

How to use this book

1. Grab a pencil and eraser.

2. Using the canvas on the right page of every monster, **LIGHTLY** draw each of the steps in order from 1 to 6 (Step 1 has already been started for you).

3. After you've finished step 5, erase all of your scratch lines to match the final drawing in step 6.

4. Take your drawing a little further by outlining it with pen or marker.

5. Now can you do it WITHOUT the starter shapes?

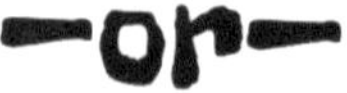

Ignore everything we've just told you and do it however you want. This is art, after all!

Loch Ness Monster

1.

2.

3.

4.

5.

Loch Ness Monster

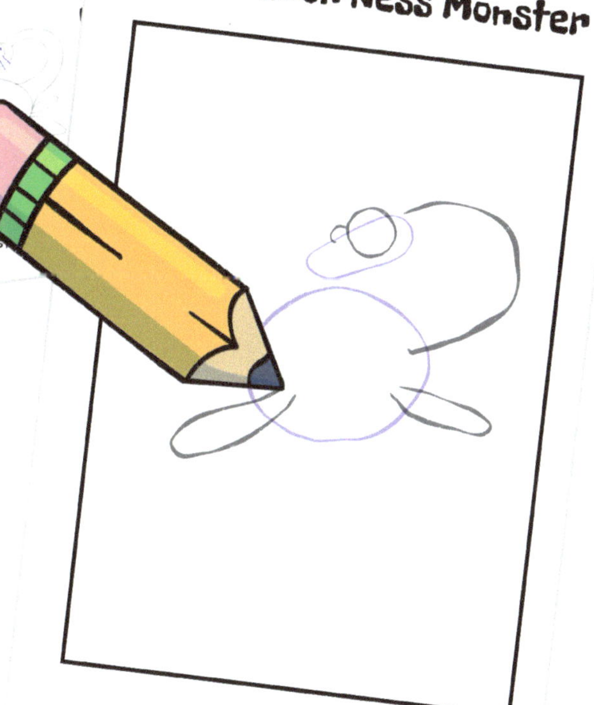

Loch Ness Monster

1.

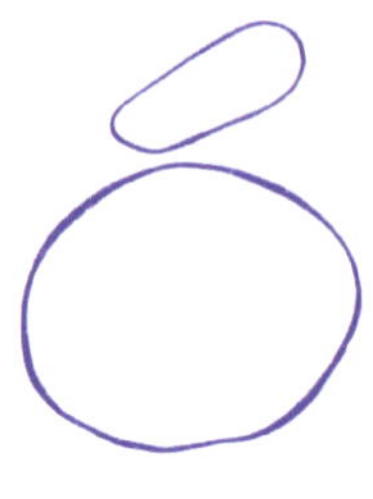

2.

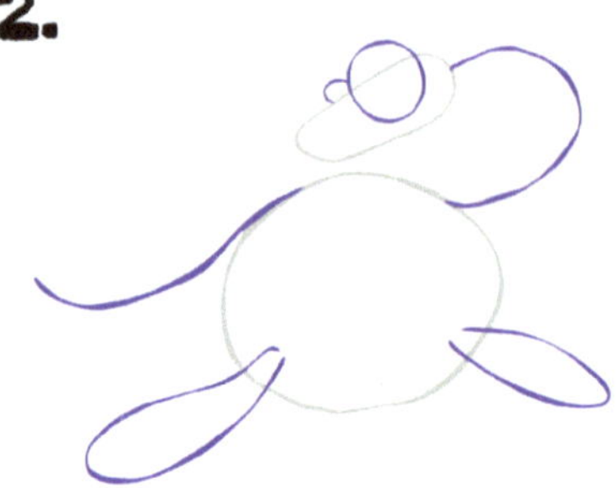

3.

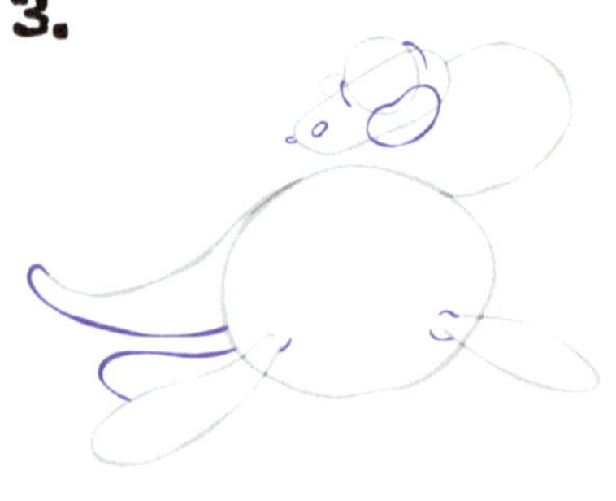

4.

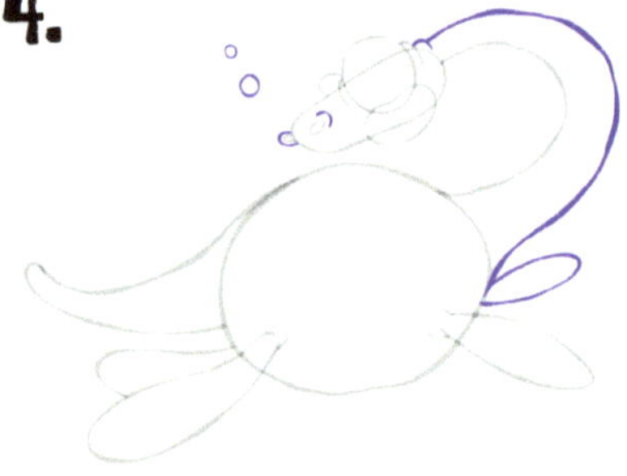

5.

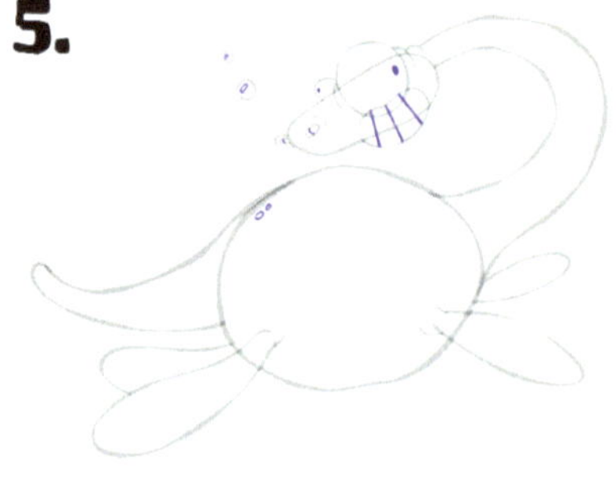

6.

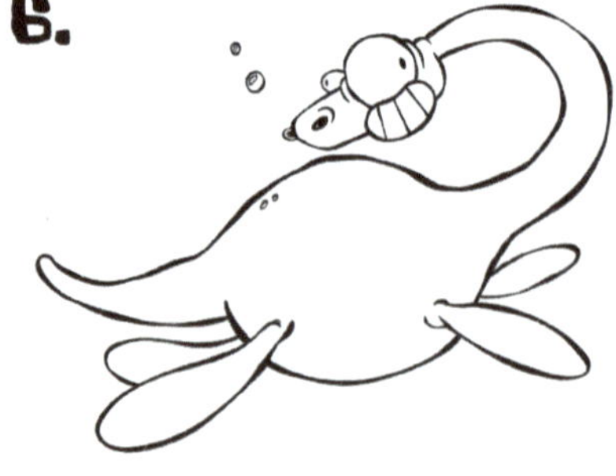

Loch Ness Monster

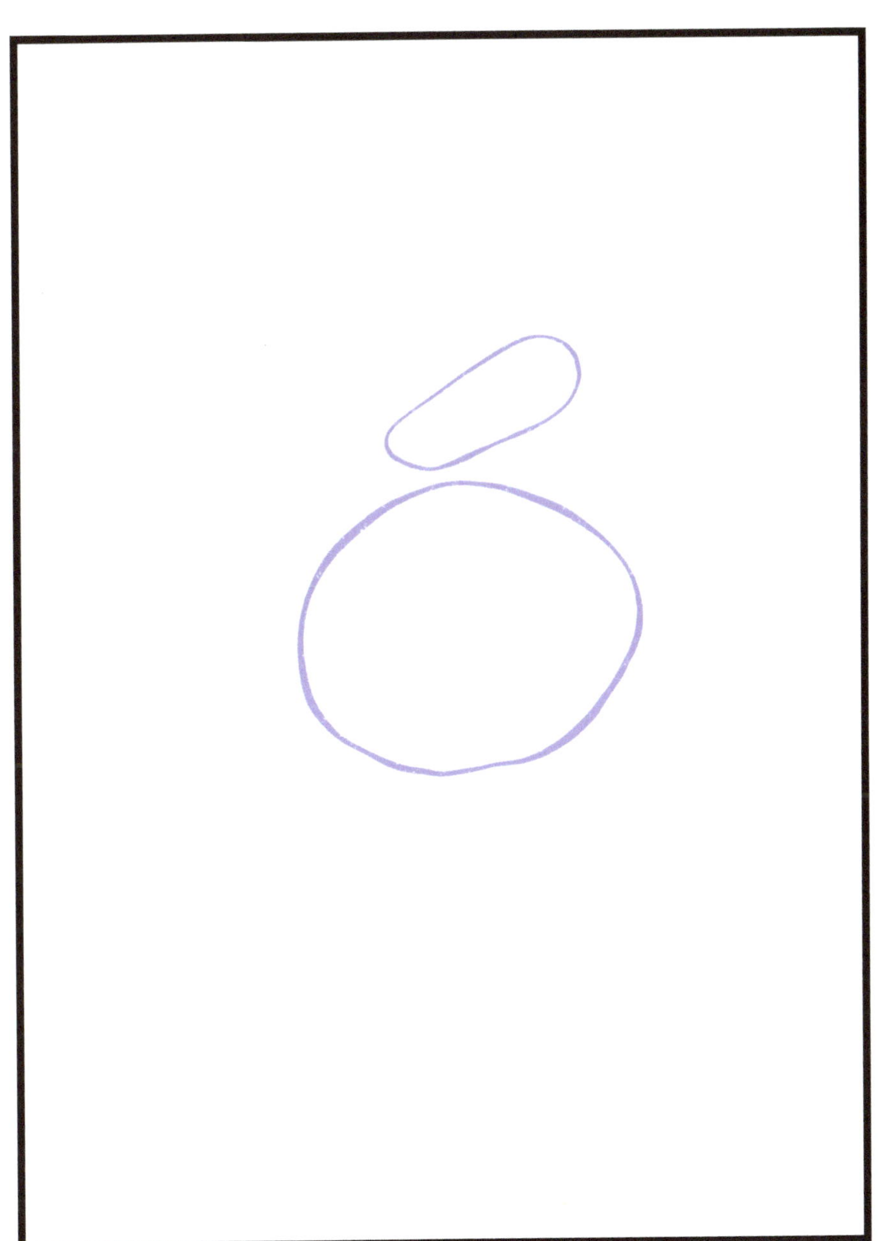

Frankenstein's Monster

1.

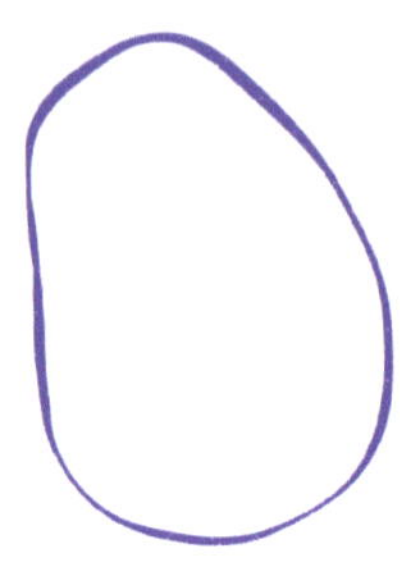

2.

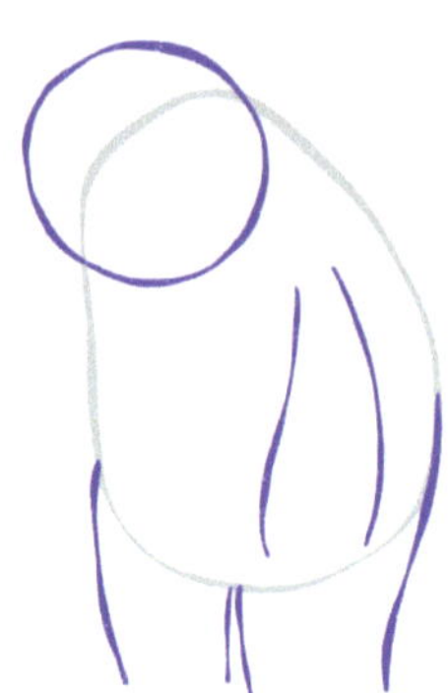

3.

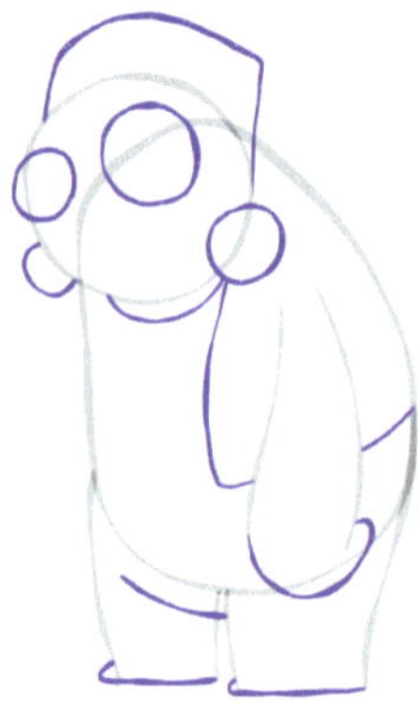

4.

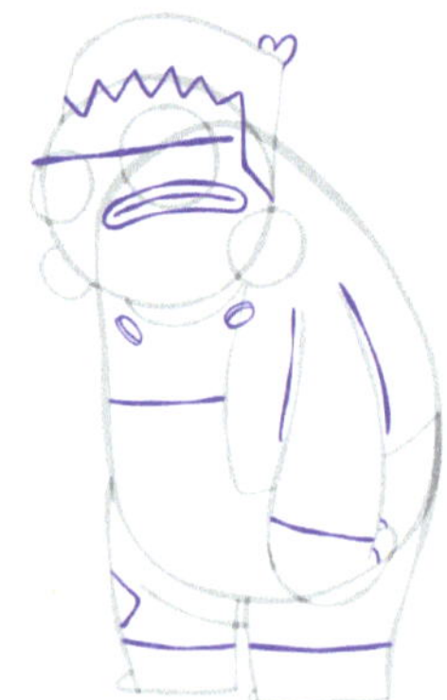

5.

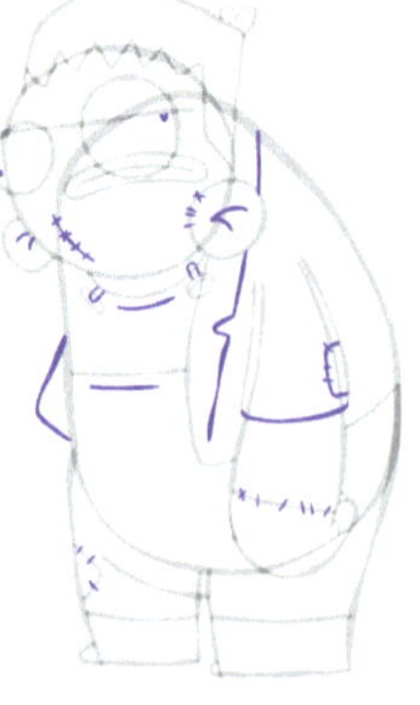

6.

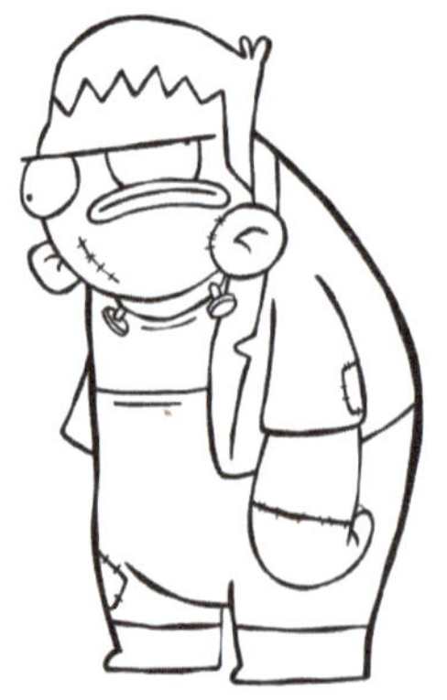

Frankenstein's Monster

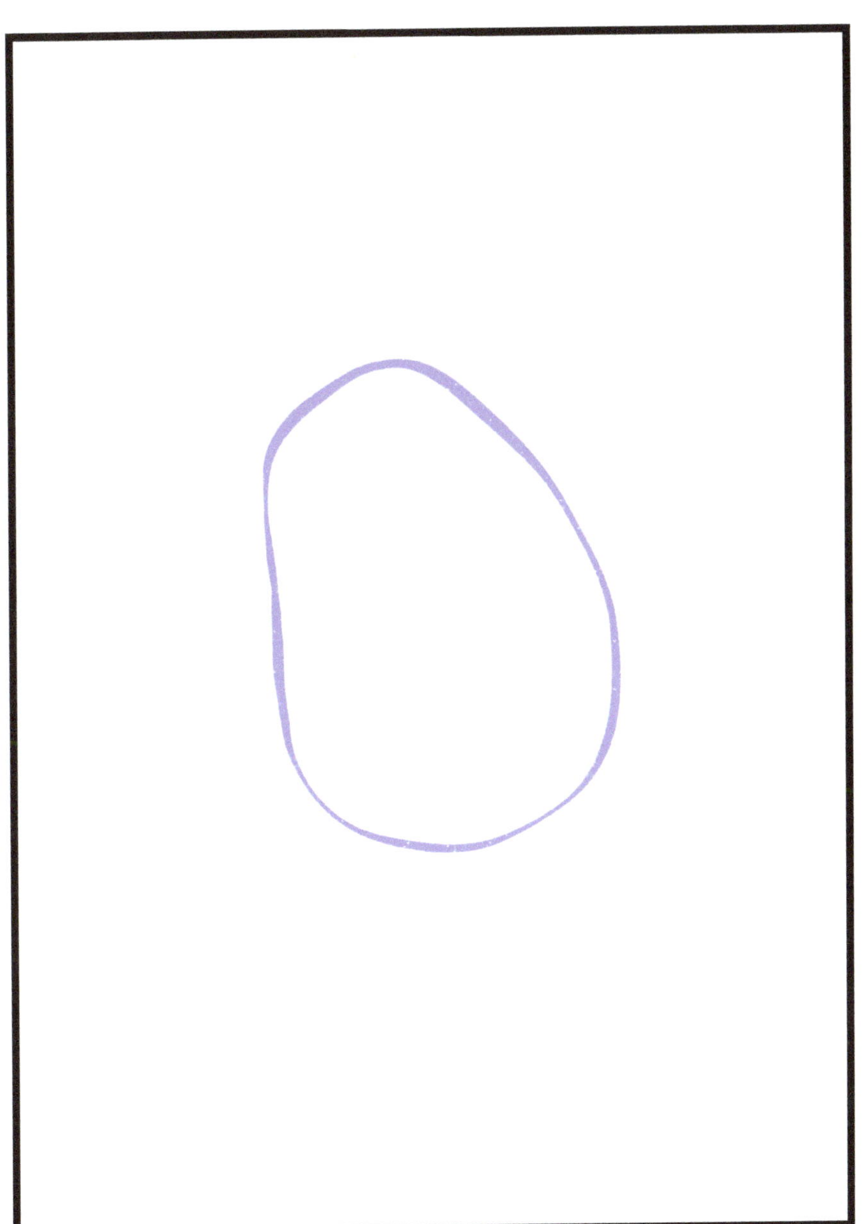

Frankenstein's Girlfriend

1.

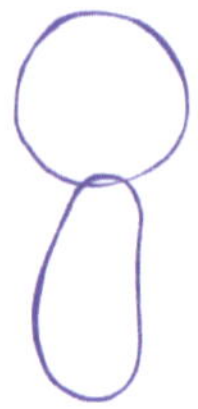

2.

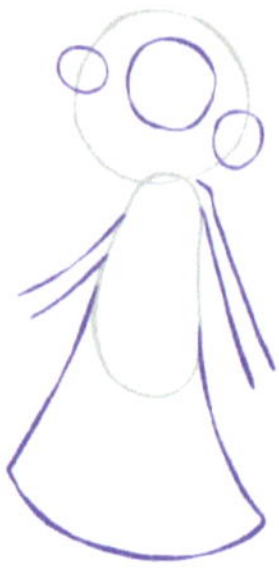

3.

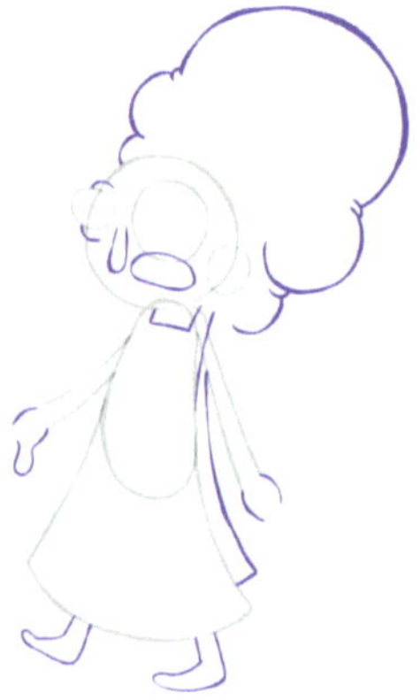

4.

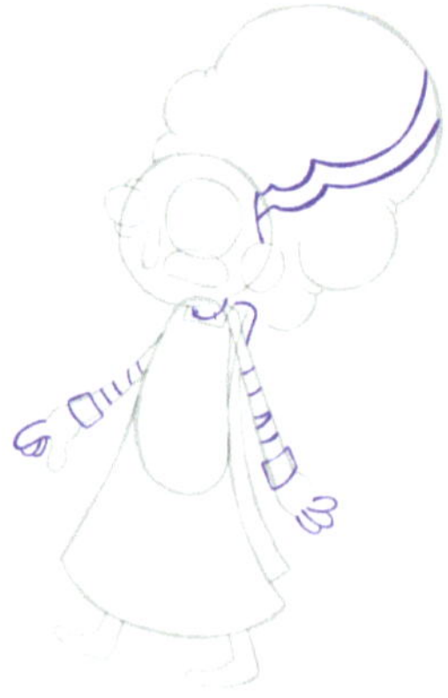

5.

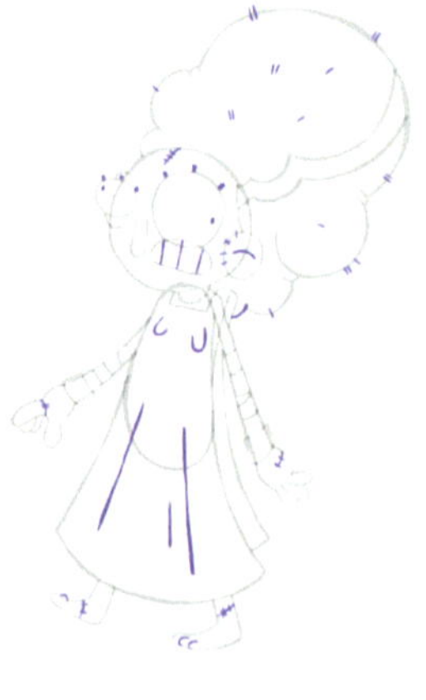

6.

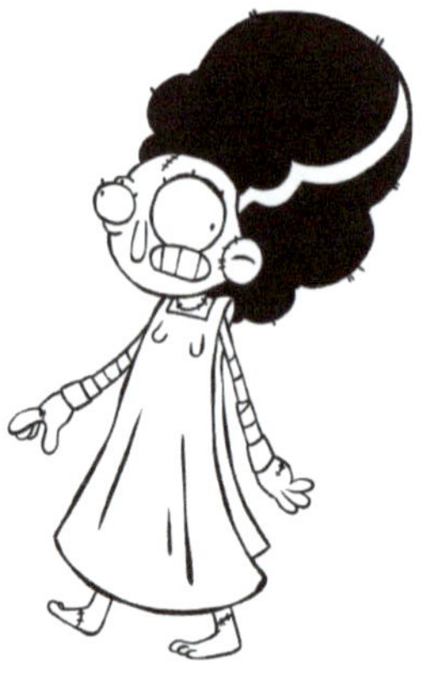

Frankenstein's Girlfriend

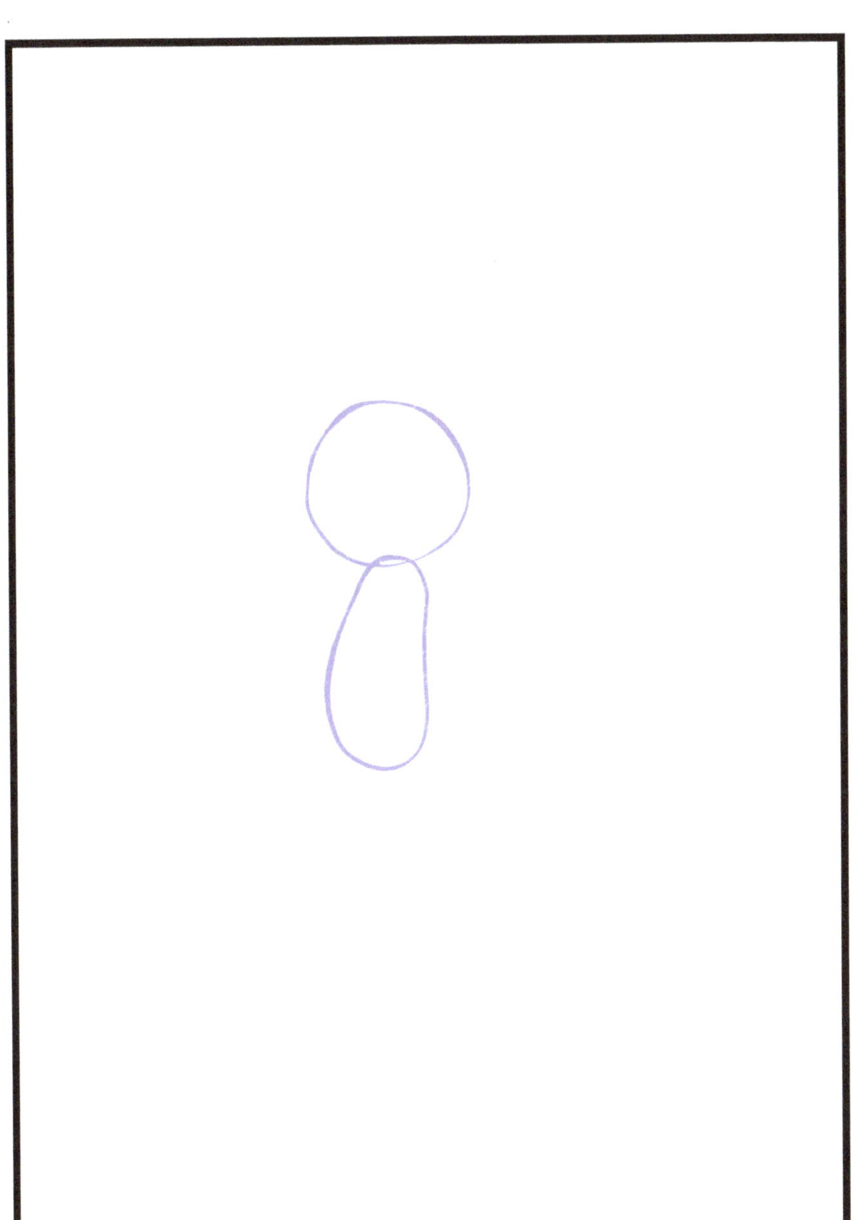

Dracula

1. 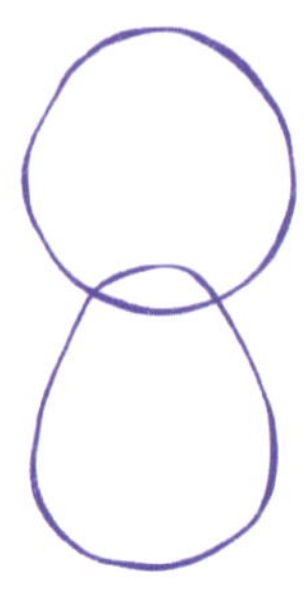

2. 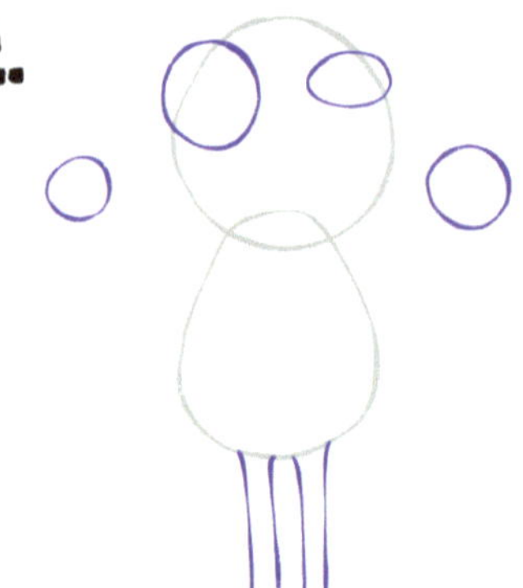

3. 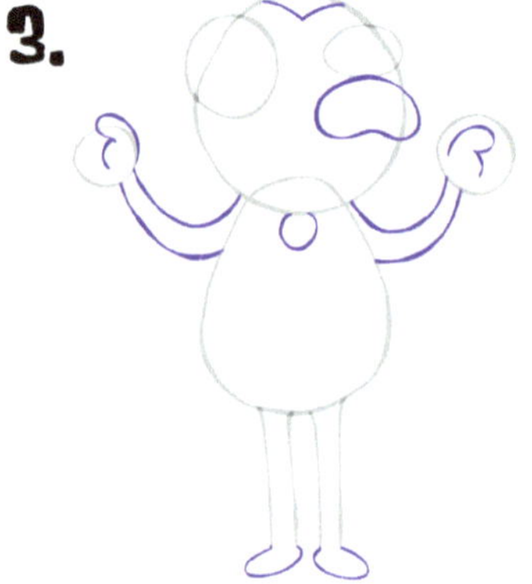

4. 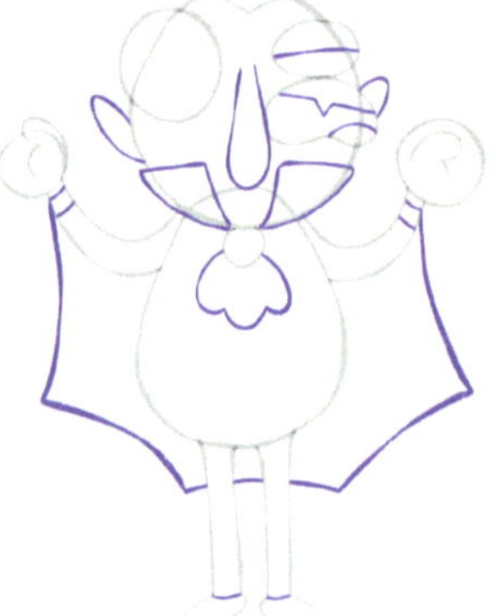

5. 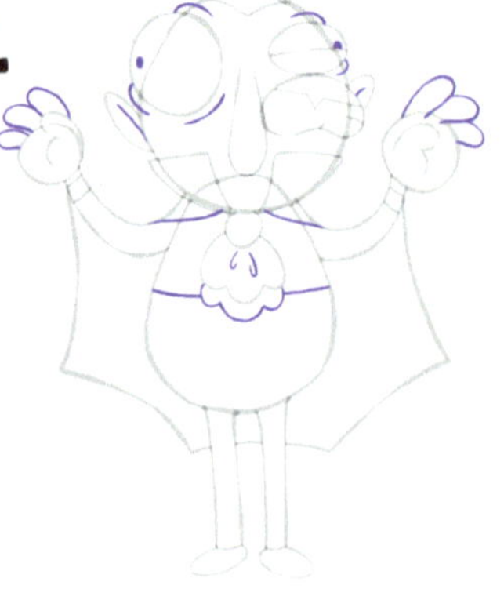

6. 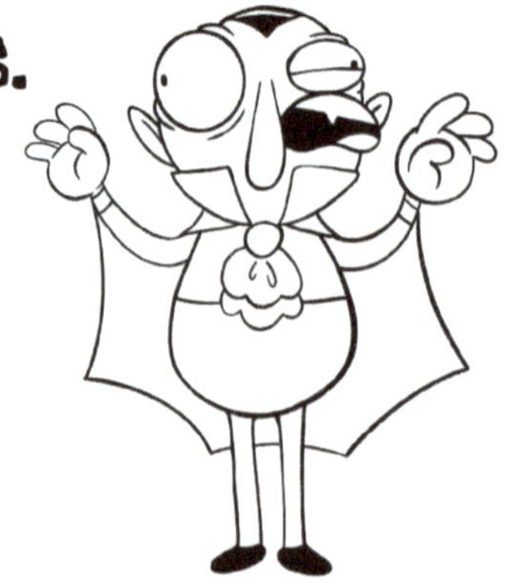

Dracula

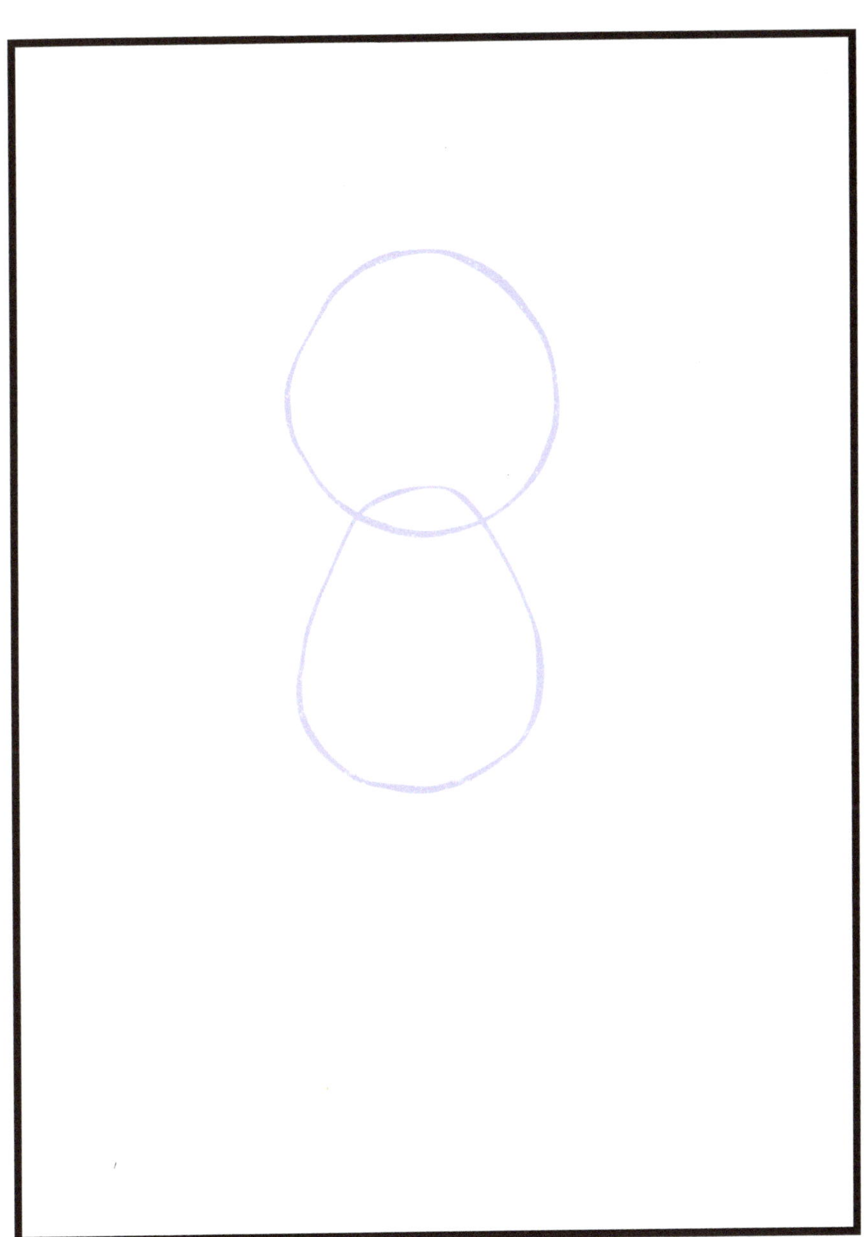

Werewolf

1.

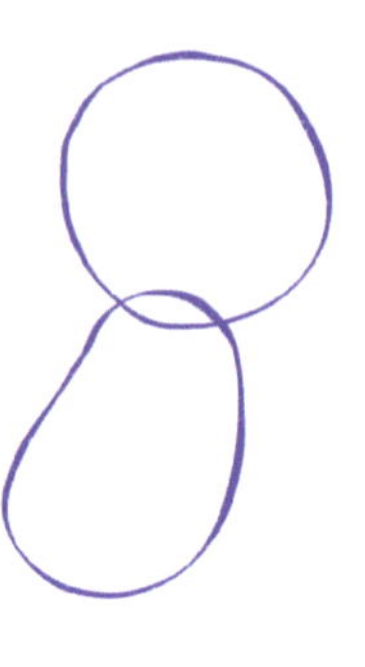

2.

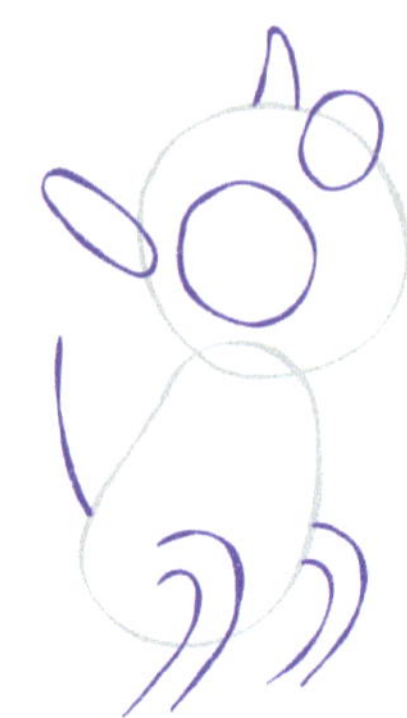

3.

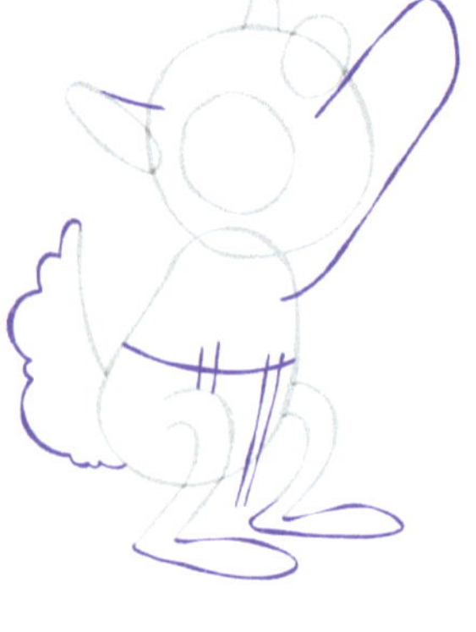

4.

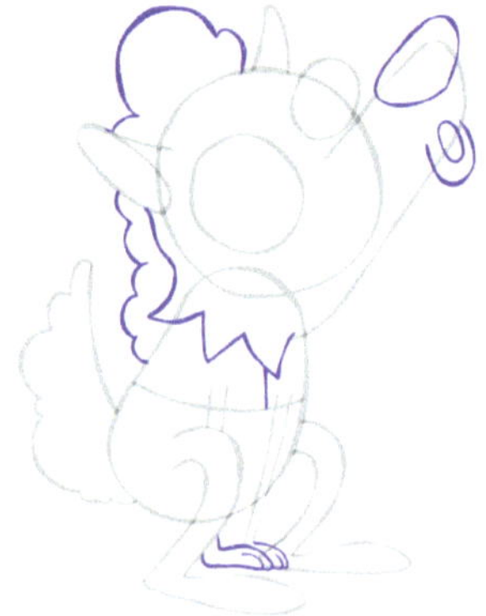

5.

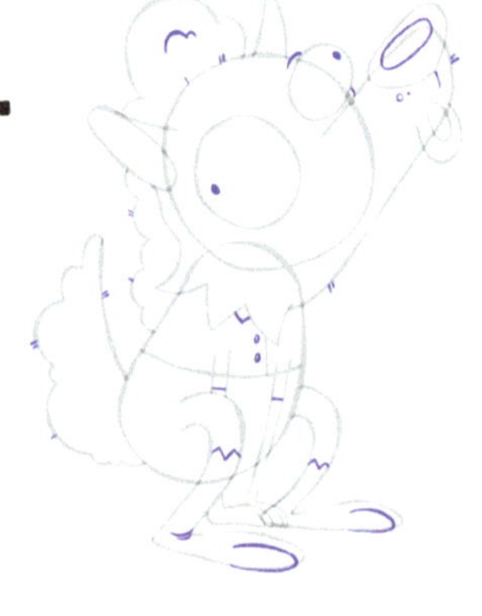

6.

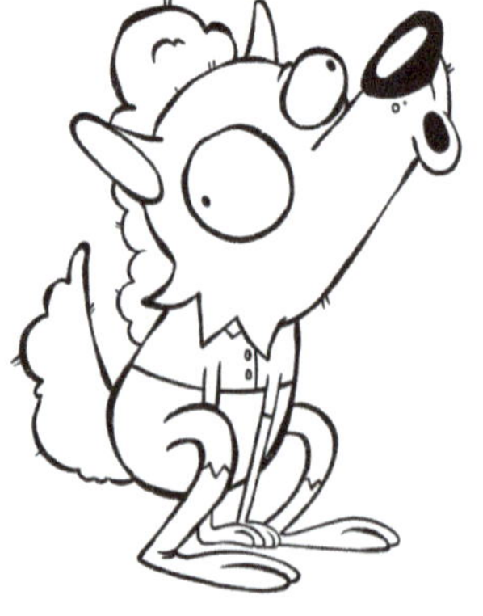

Werewolf

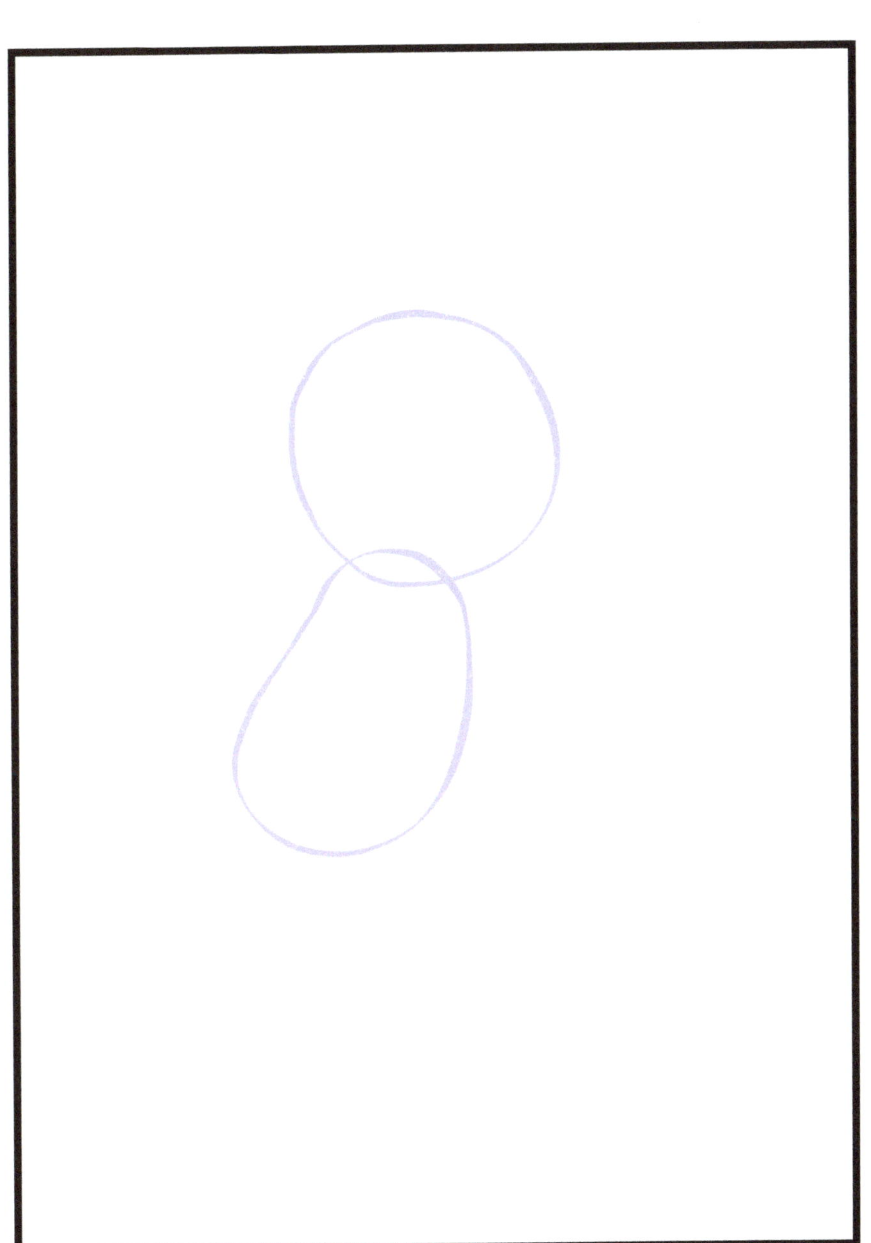

Mummy

1.
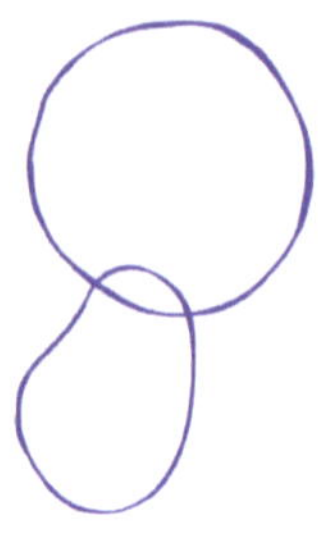

2.
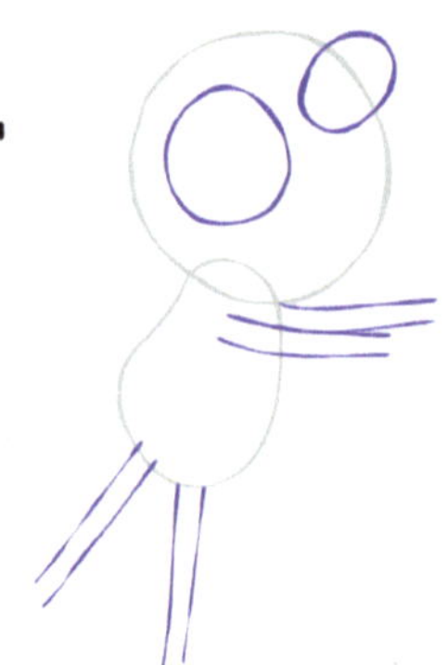

3.
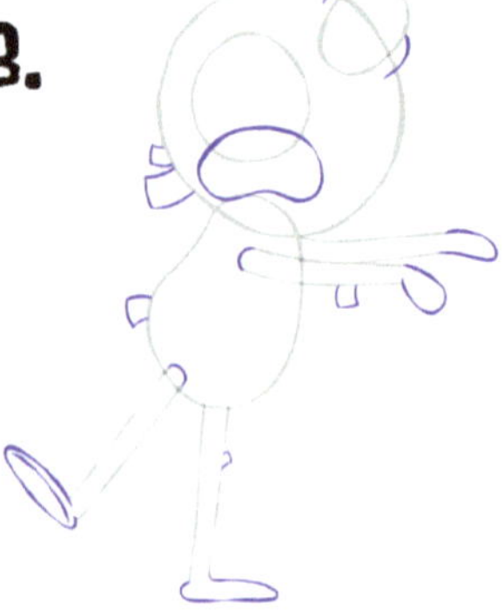

4.
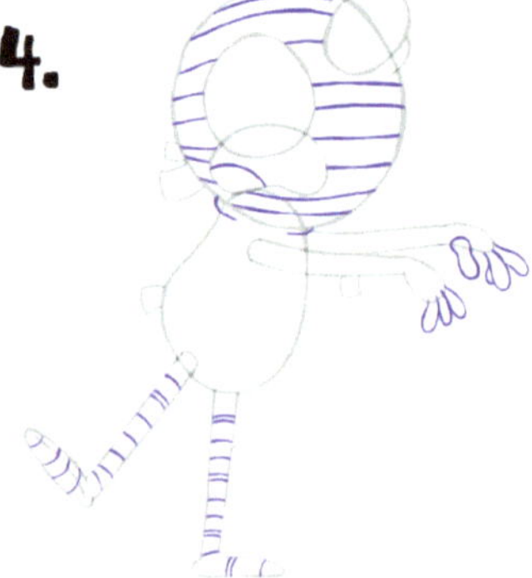

5.
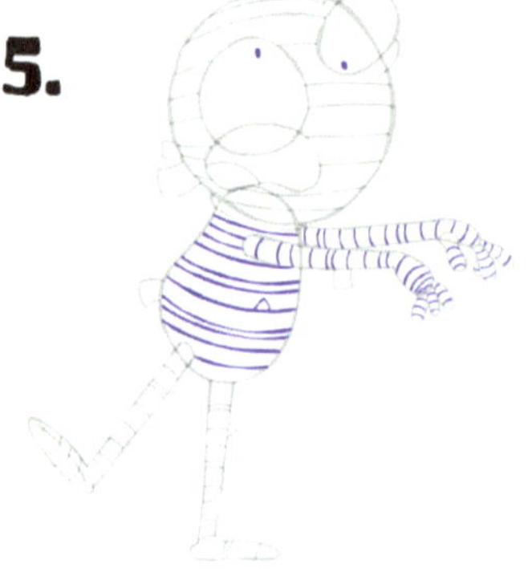

6.
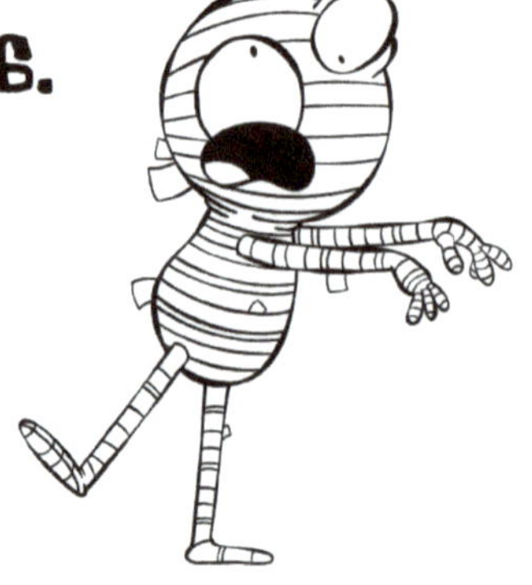

Mummy

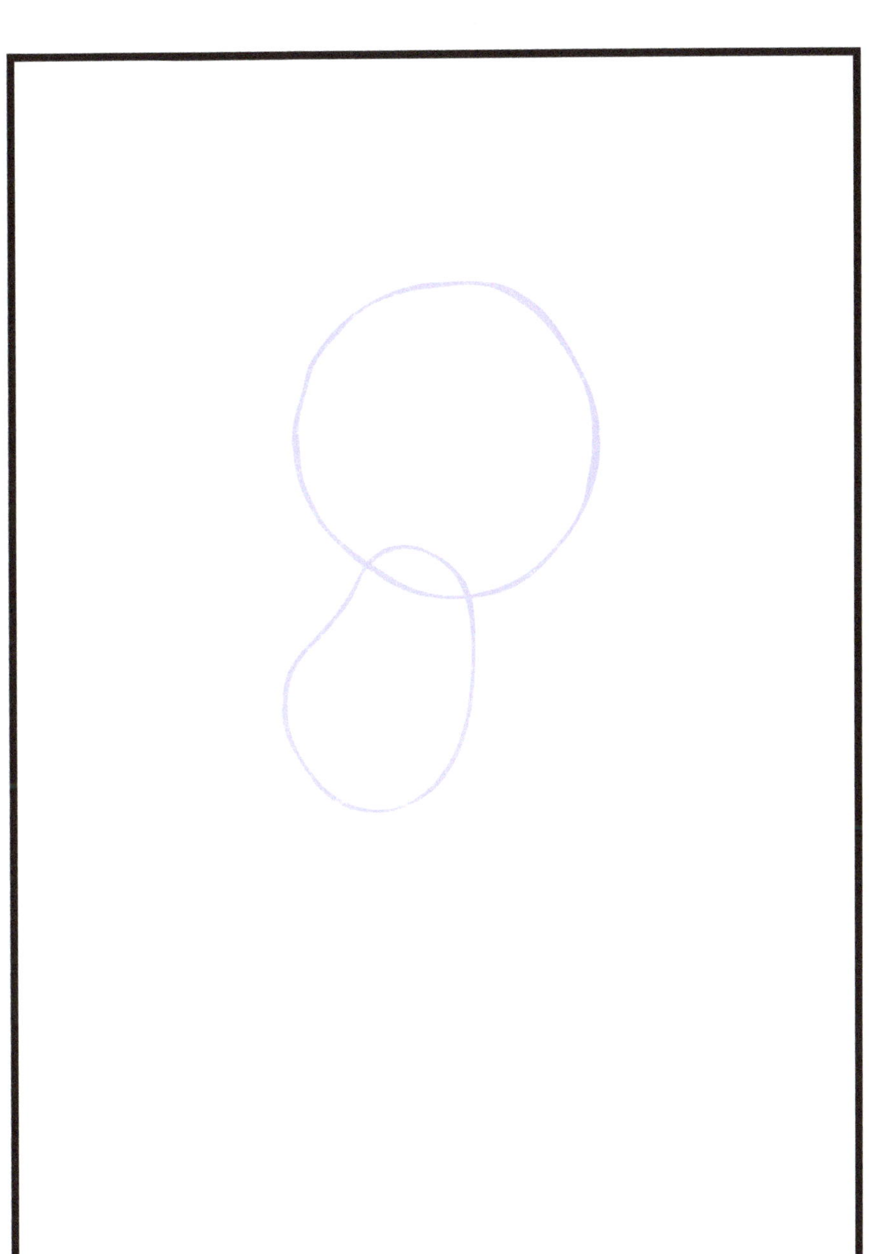

Zombie

1. 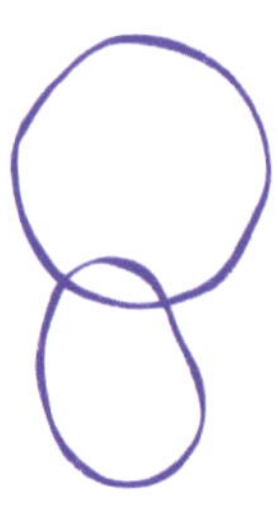

2. 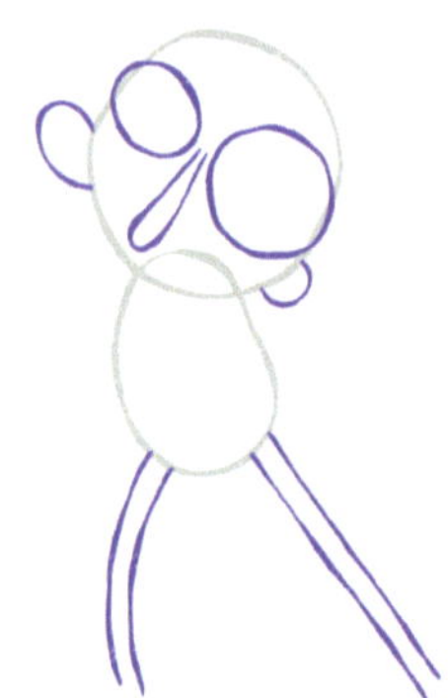

3. 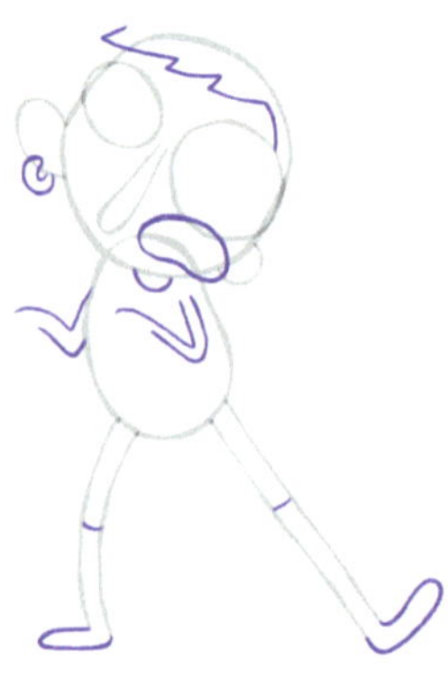

4. 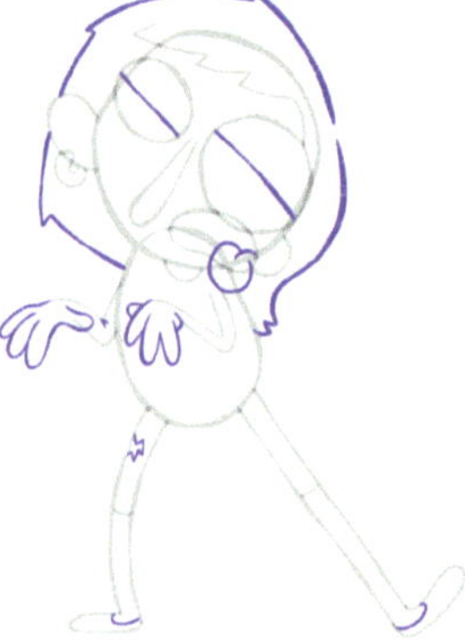

5. 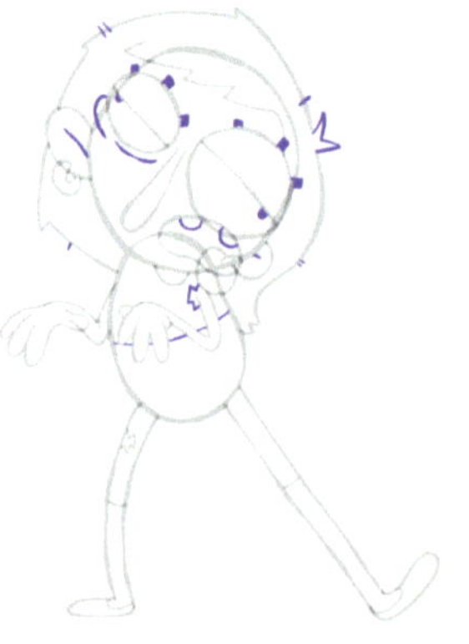

6. 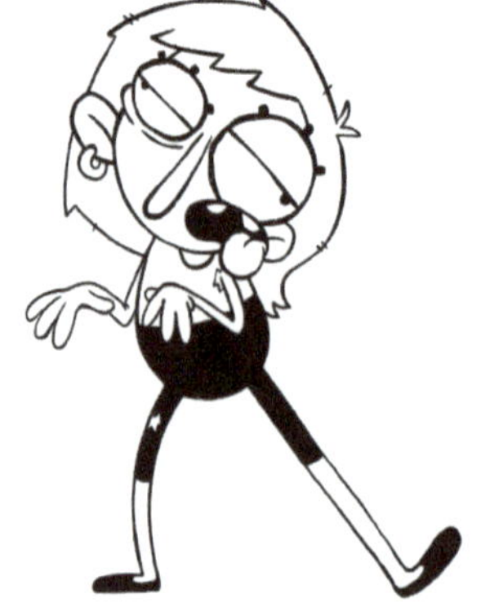

Zombie

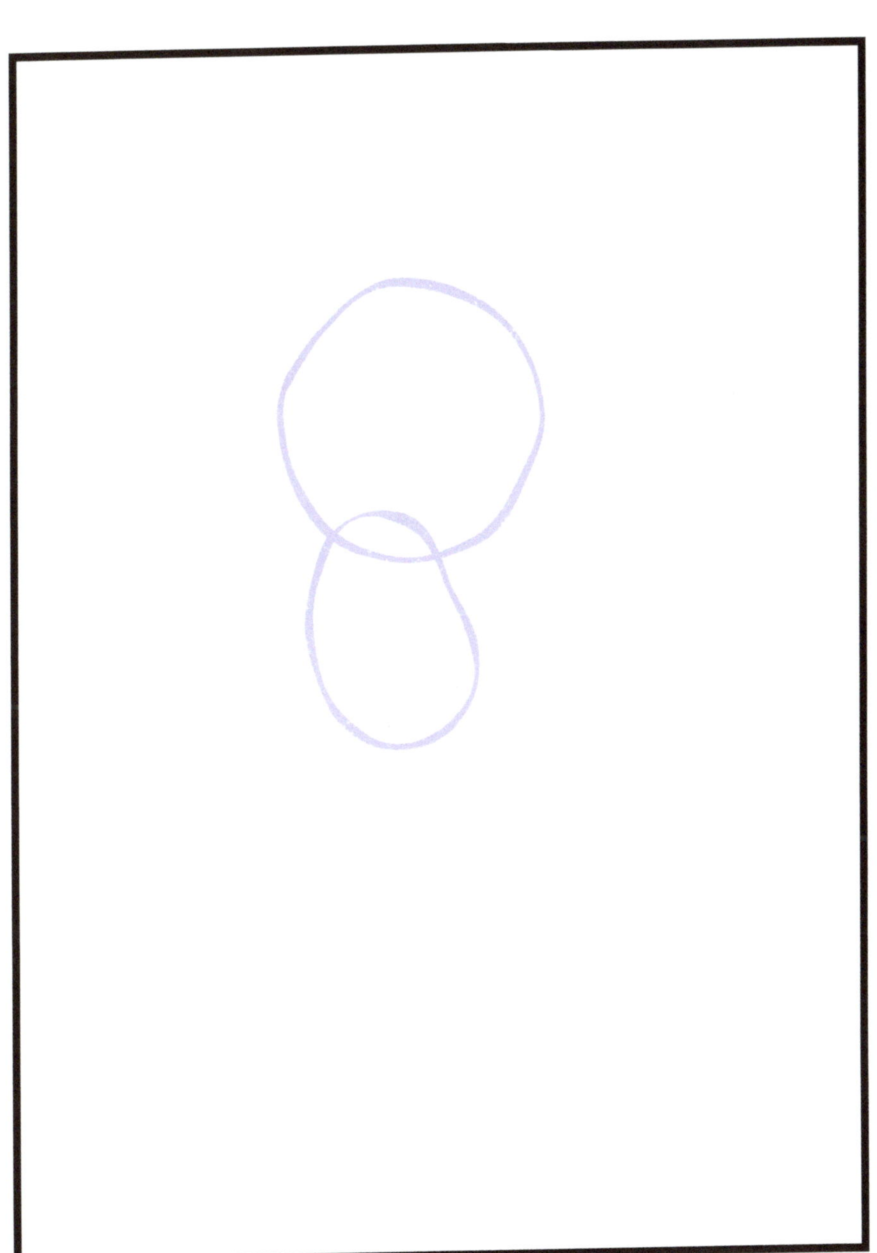

Ghost

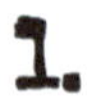

1. 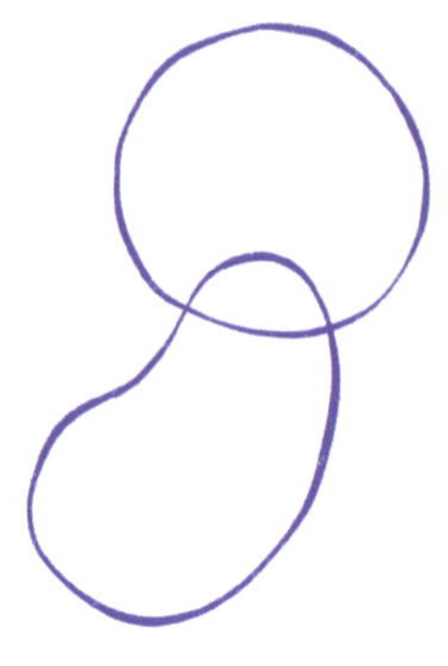

2. 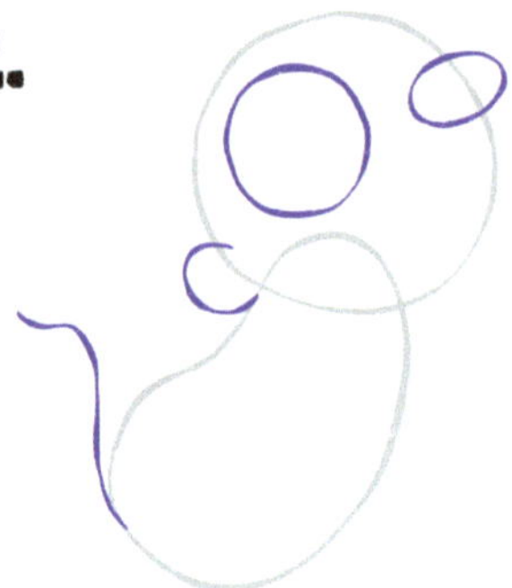

3. 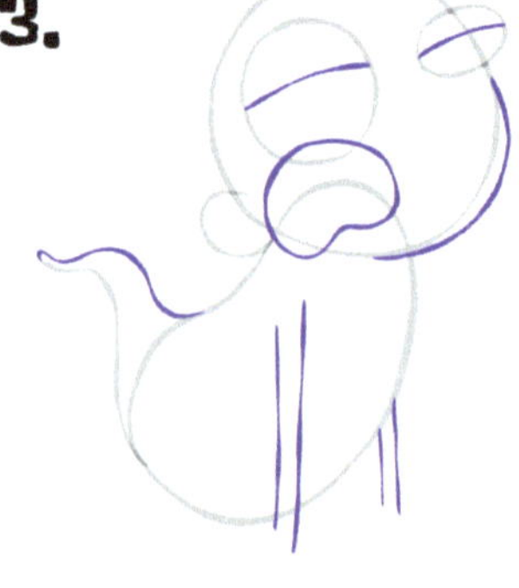

4. 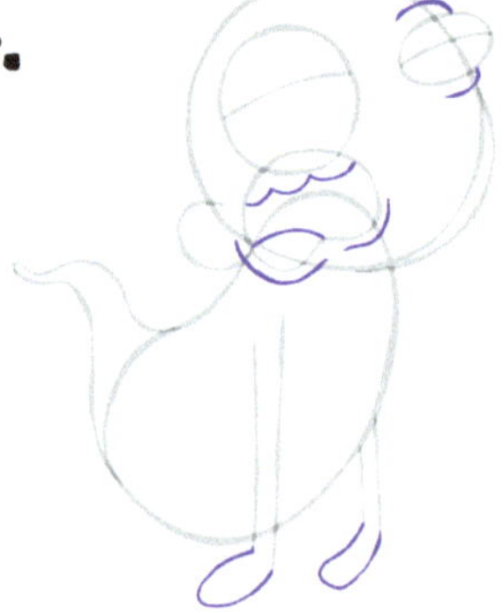

5. 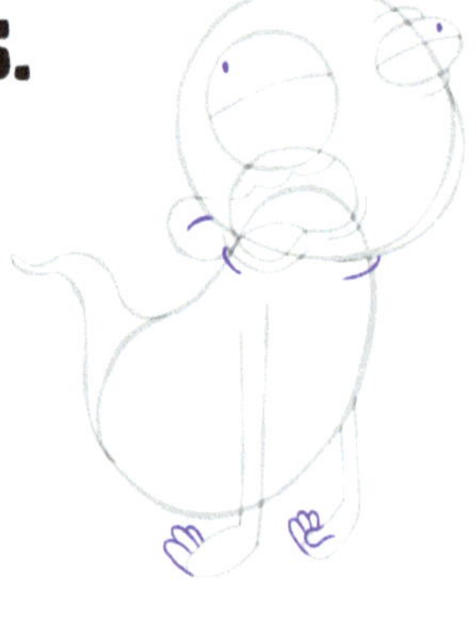

6. 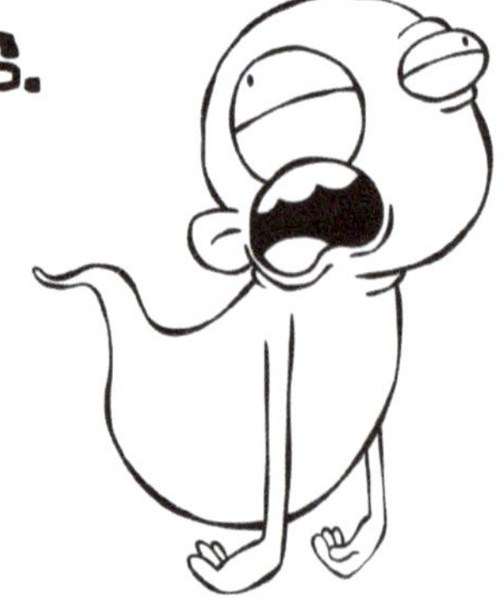

Ghost

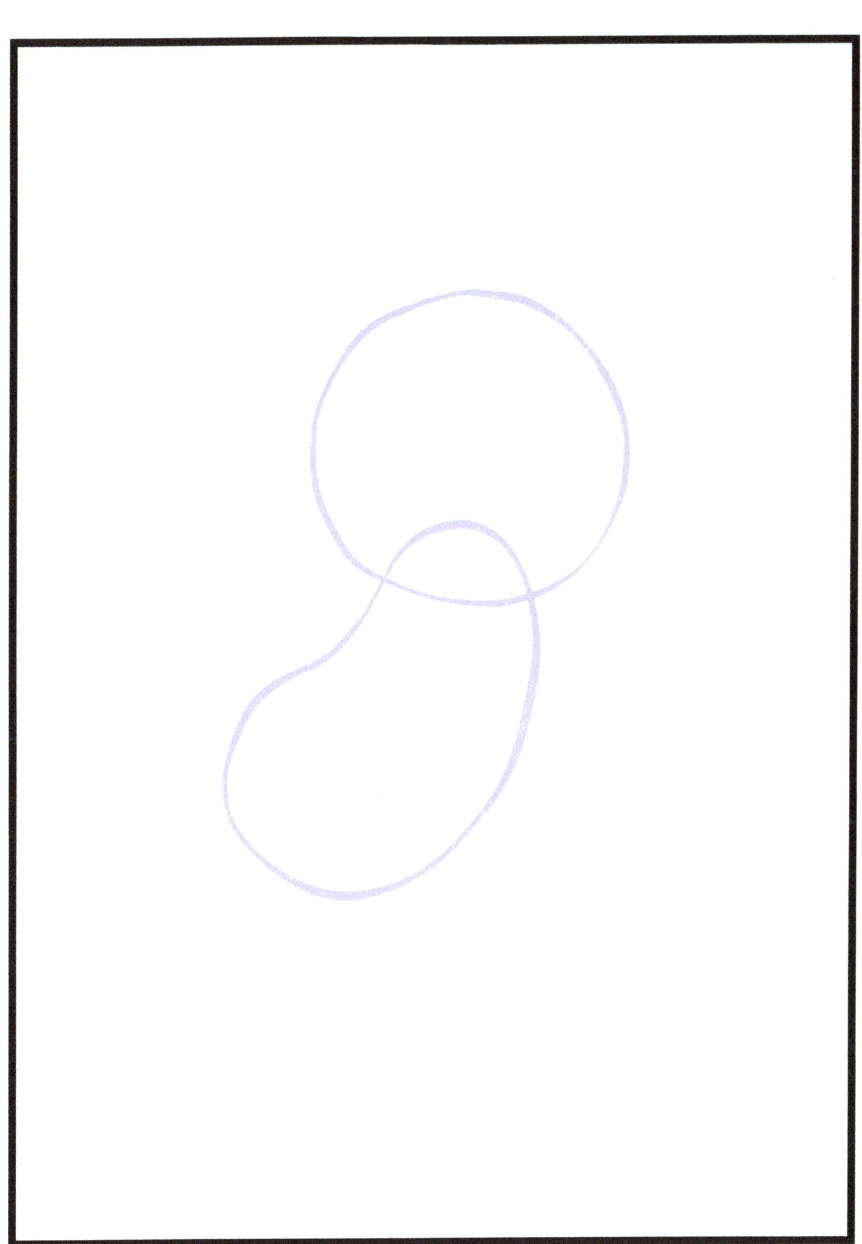

Skeleton

1. 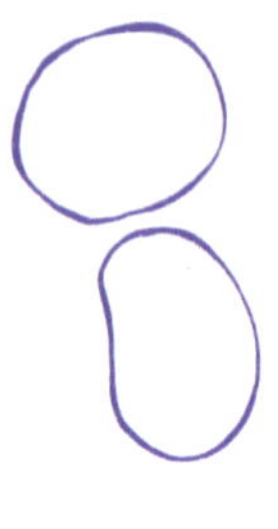

2. 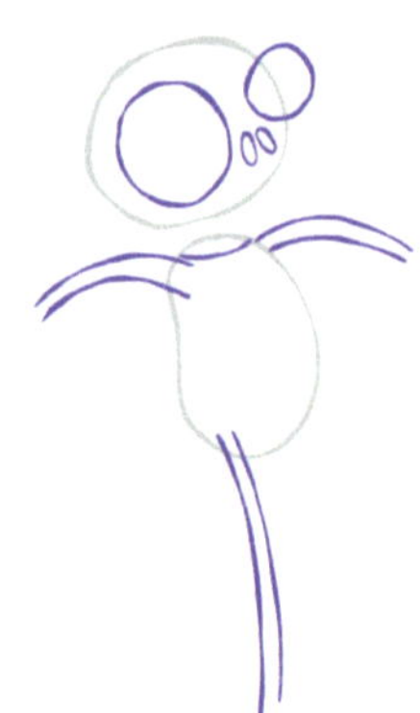

3. 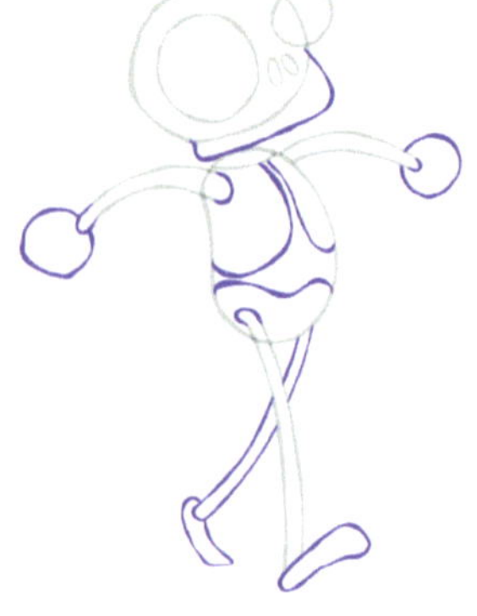

4. 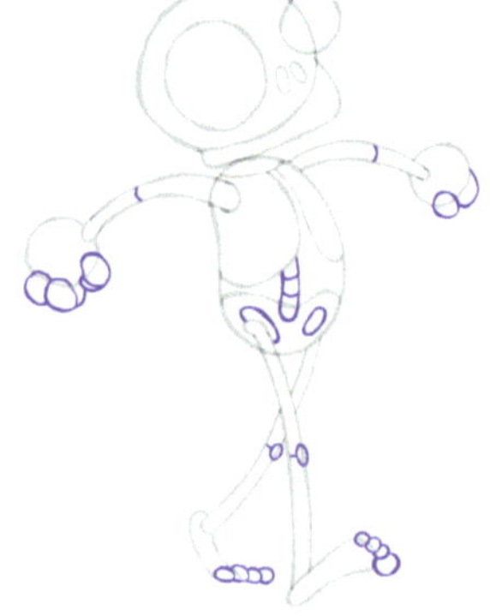

5. 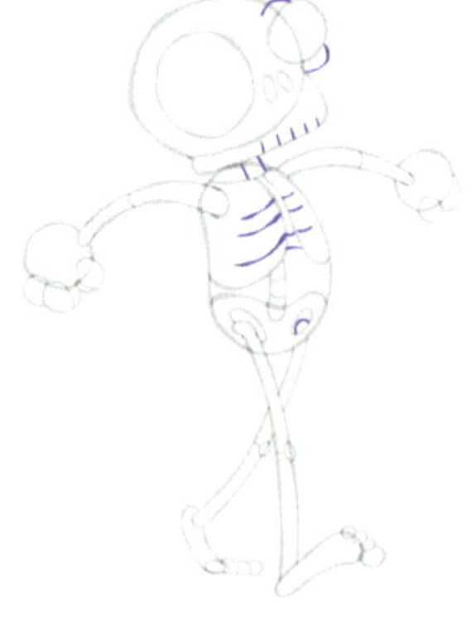

6. 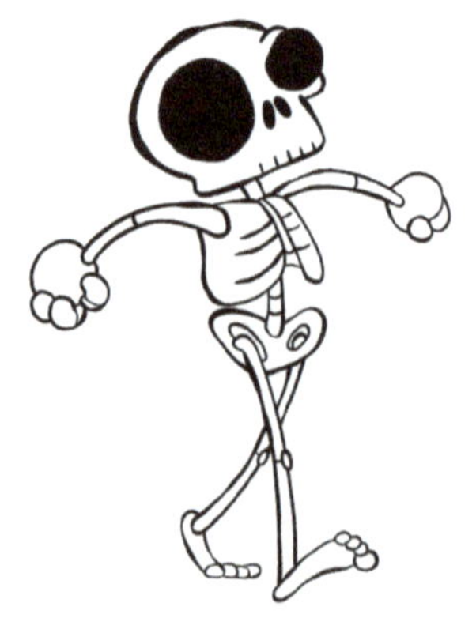

Skeleton

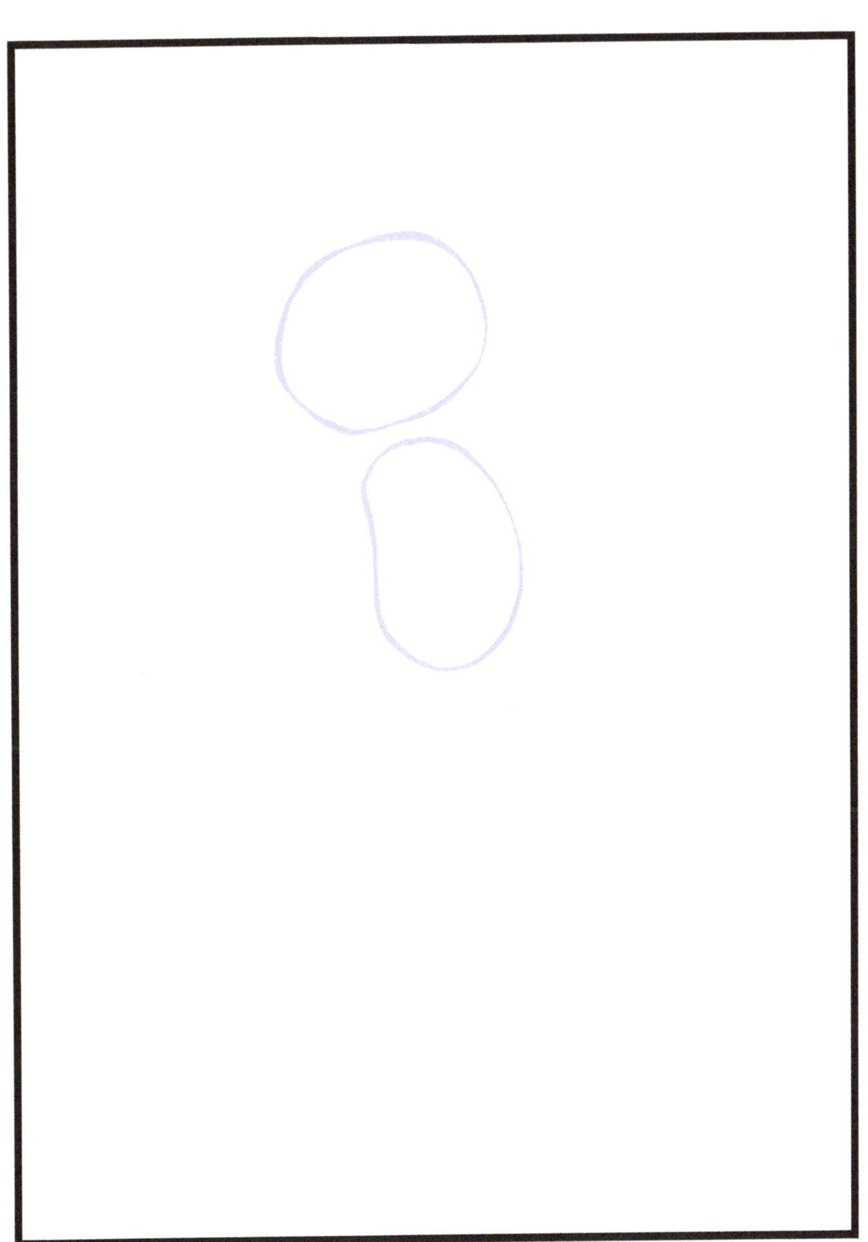

Witch

1.

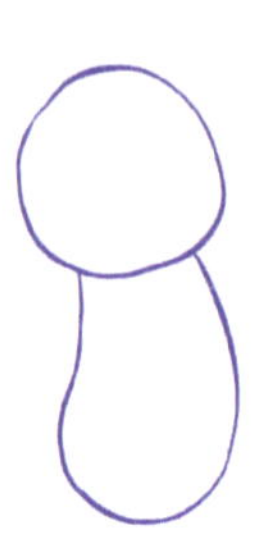

2.

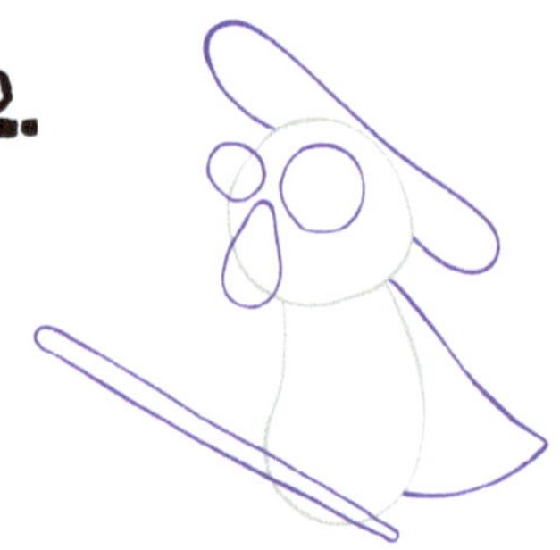

3.

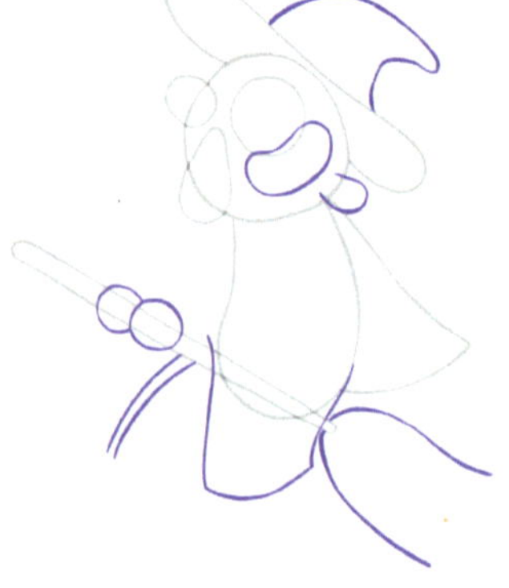

4.

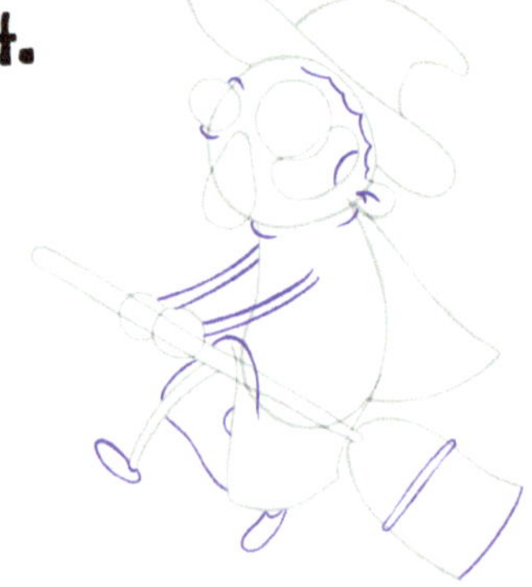

5.

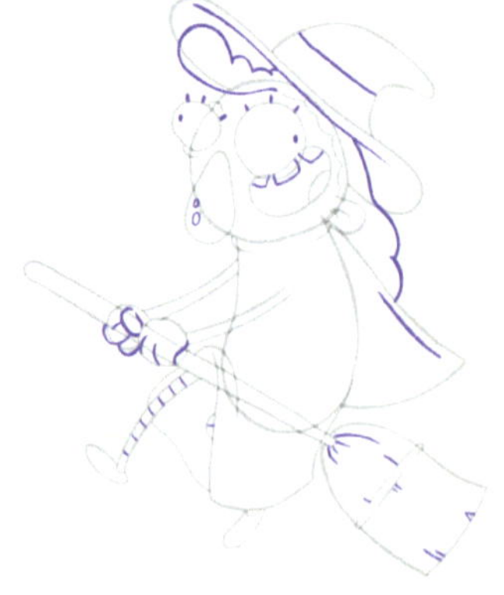

6.

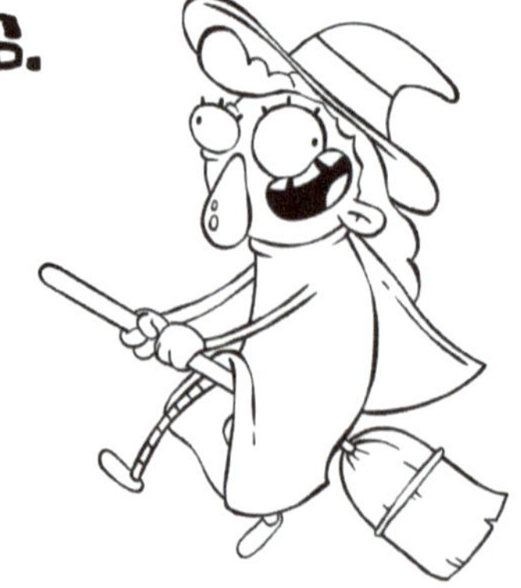

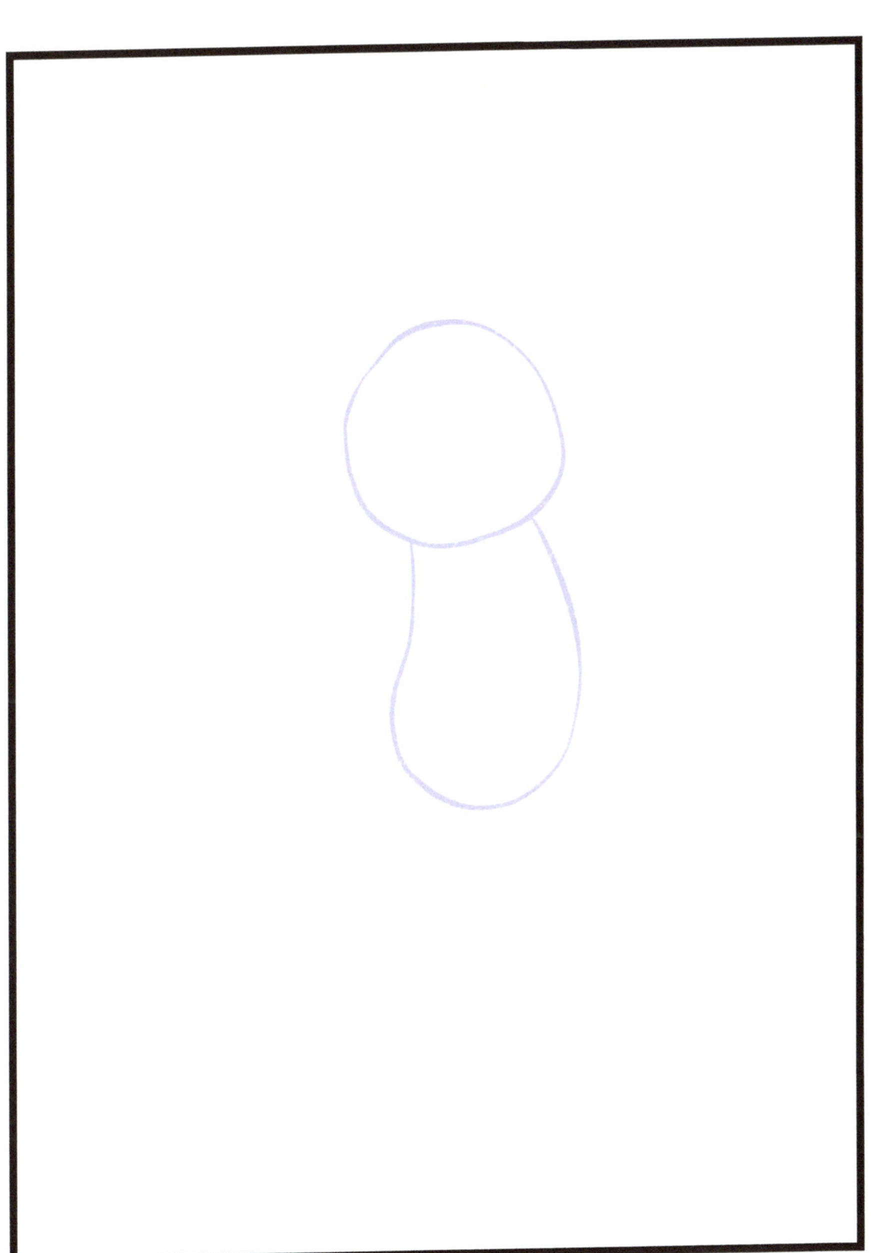

Ogre

1.

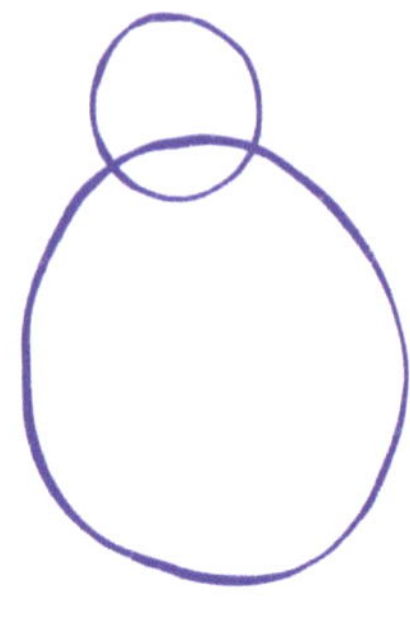

2.

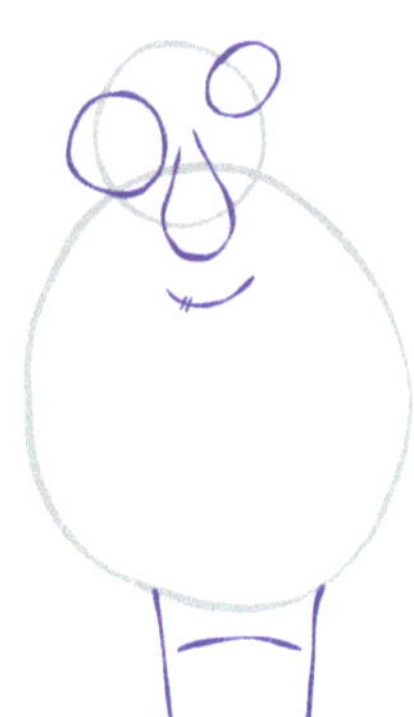

3.

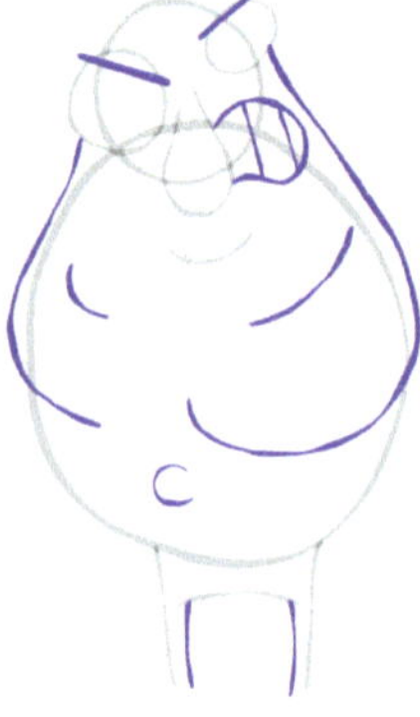

4.

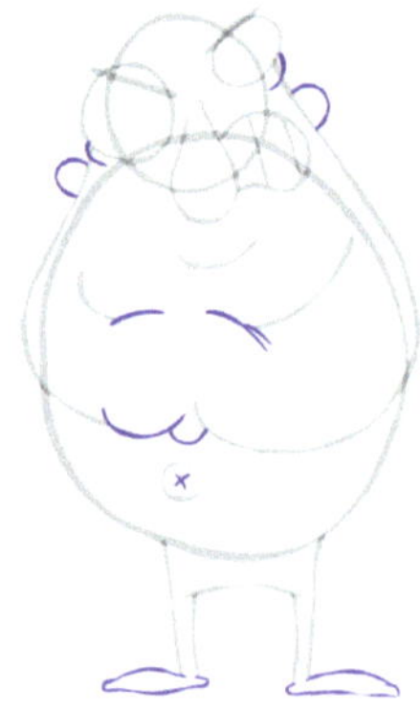

5.

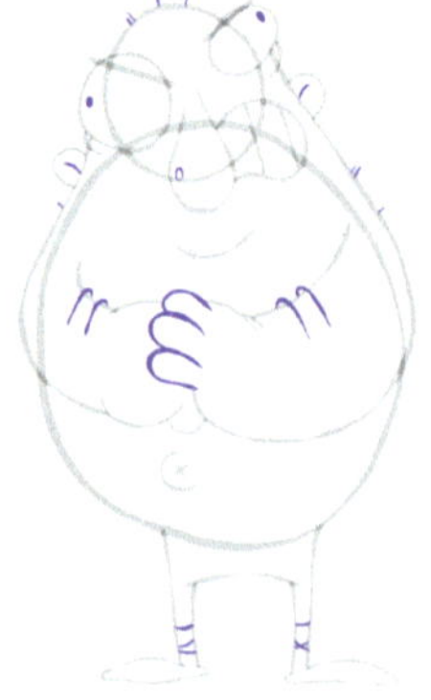

6.

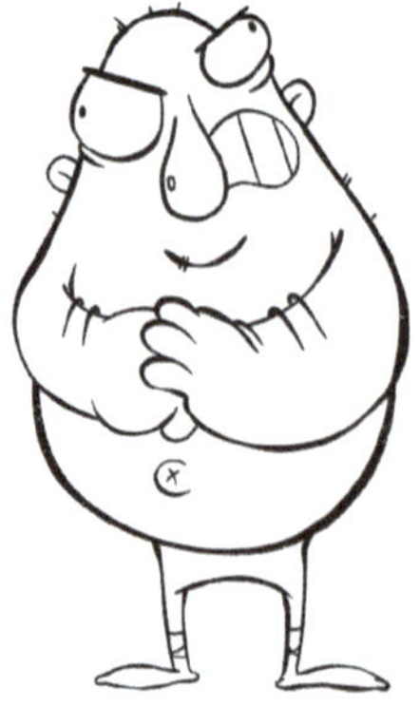

26 – Ogre

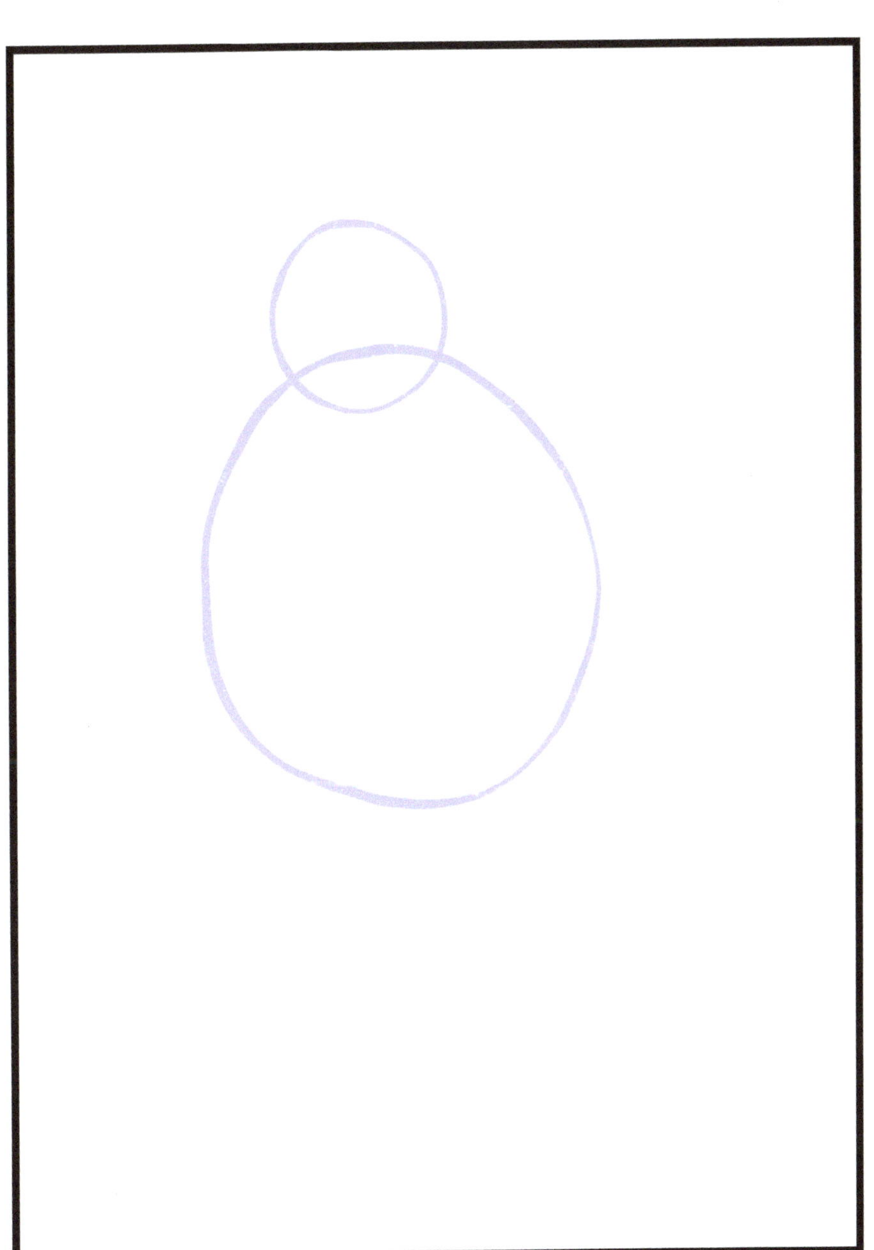

Troll

1.

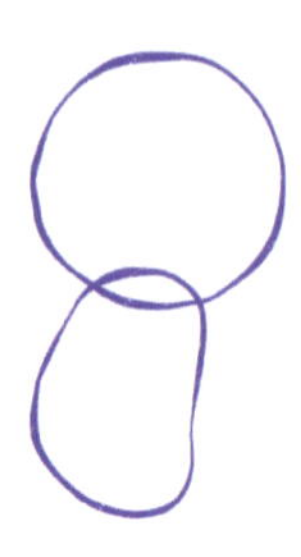

2.

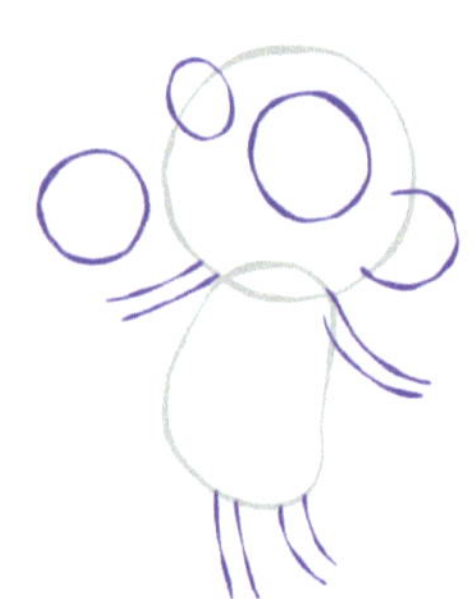

3.

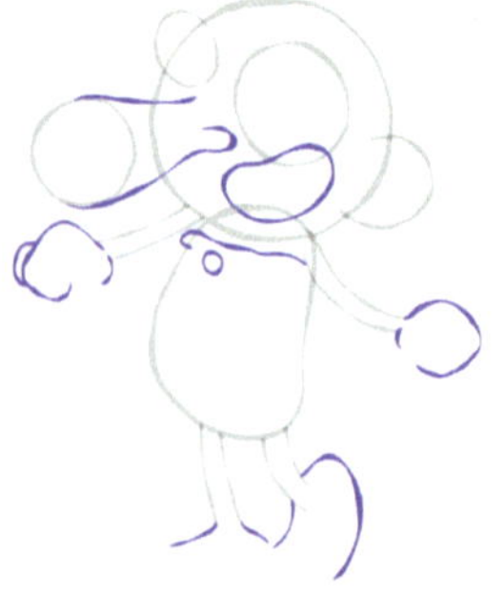

4.

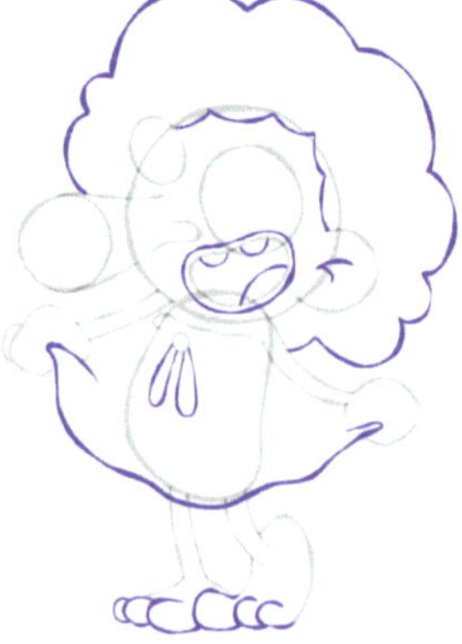

5.

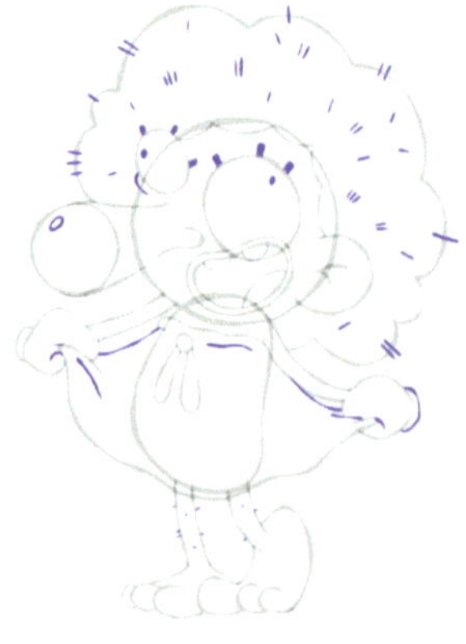

6.

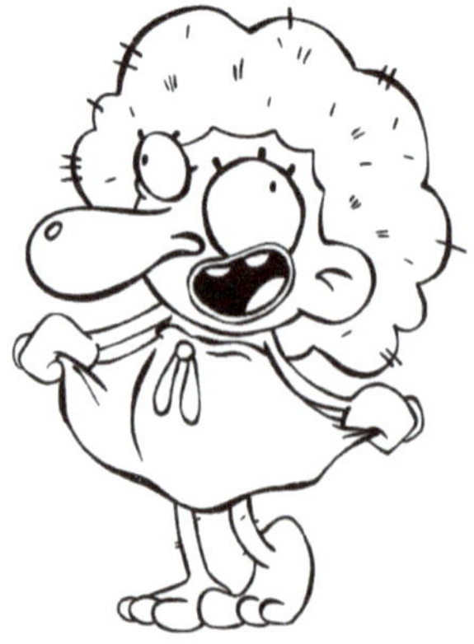

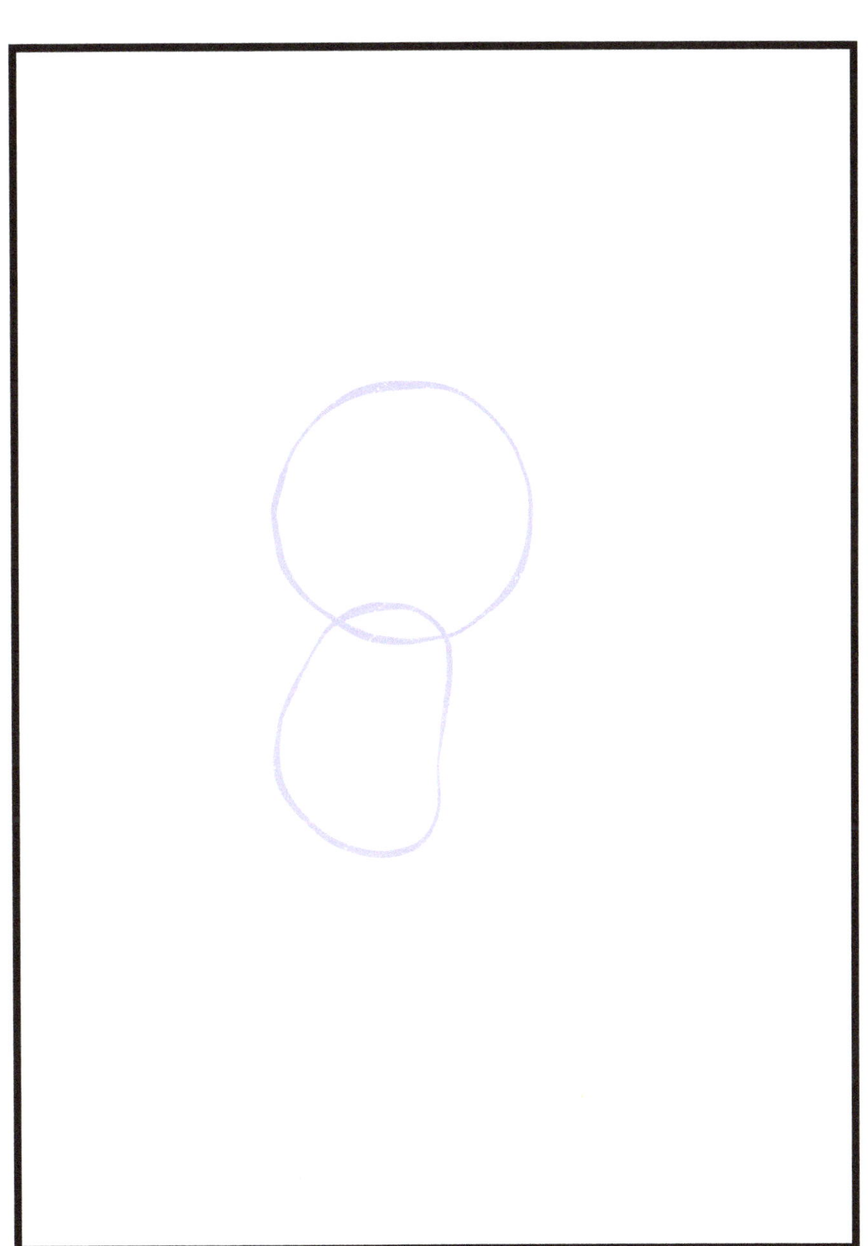

Blob

1.
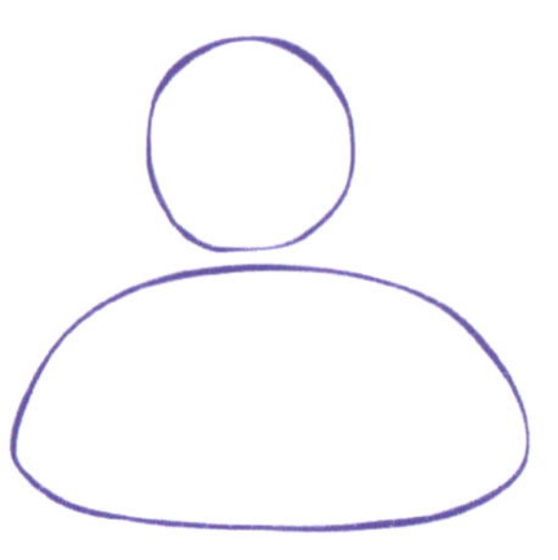

2.
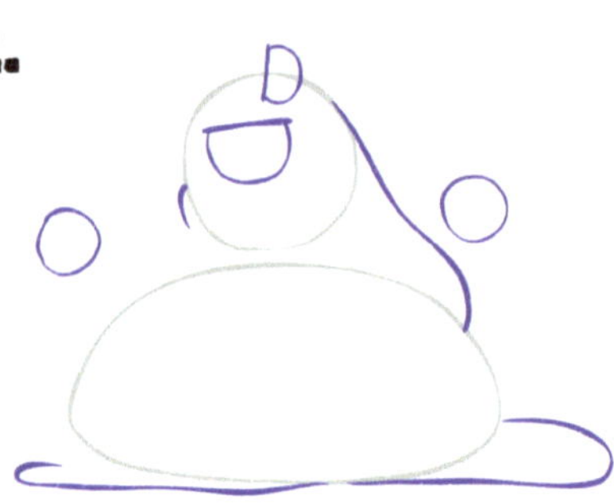

3.
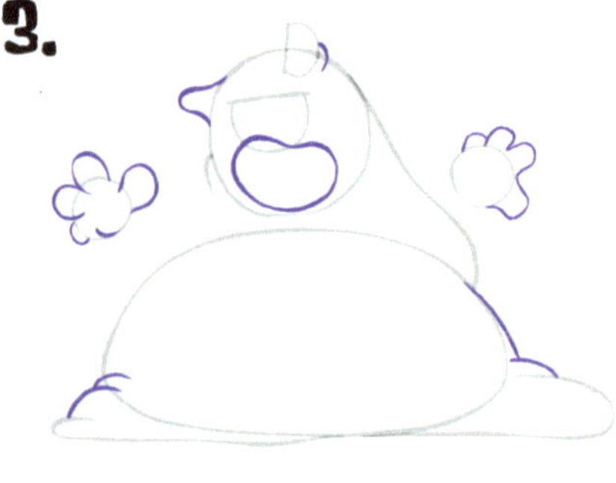

4.
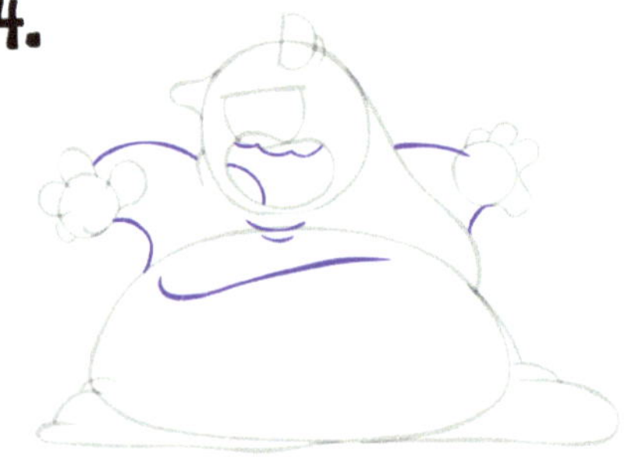

5.
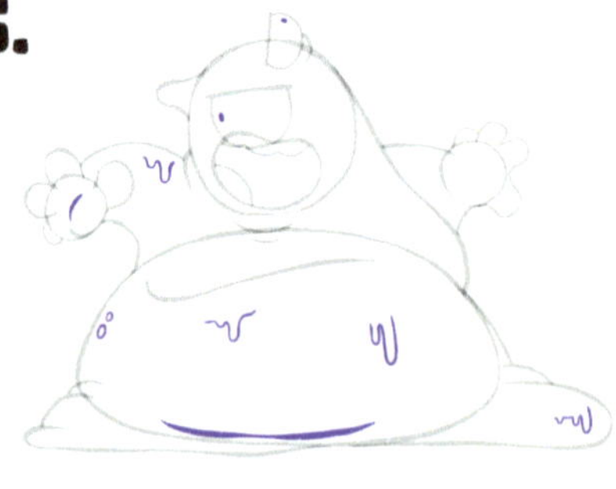

6.
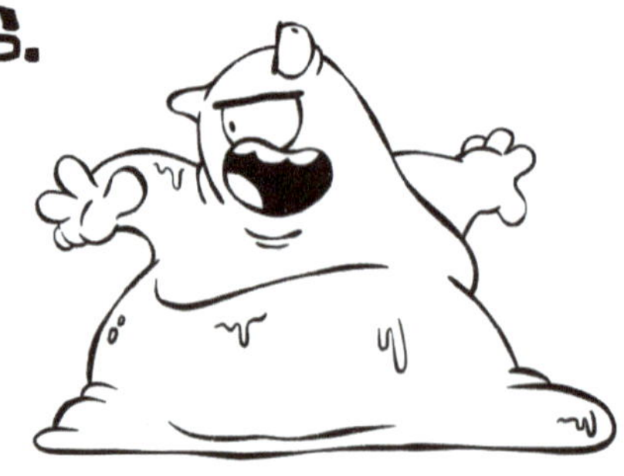

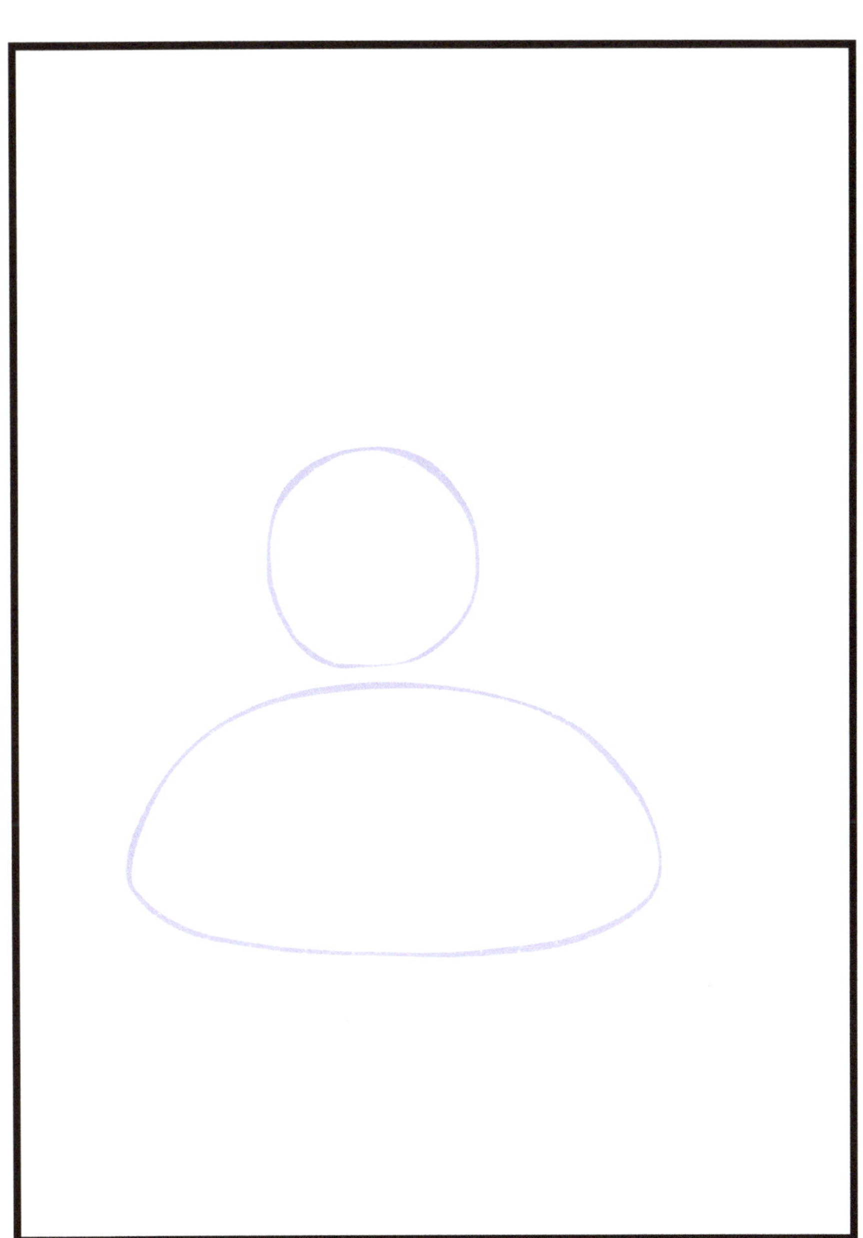

Kraken

1. 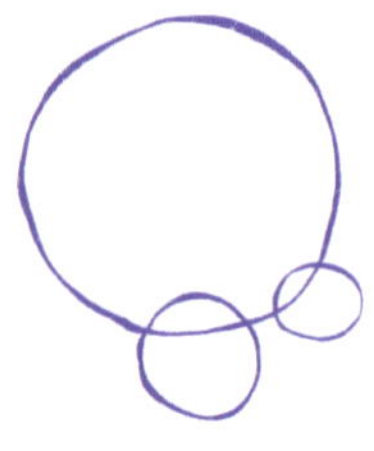

2. 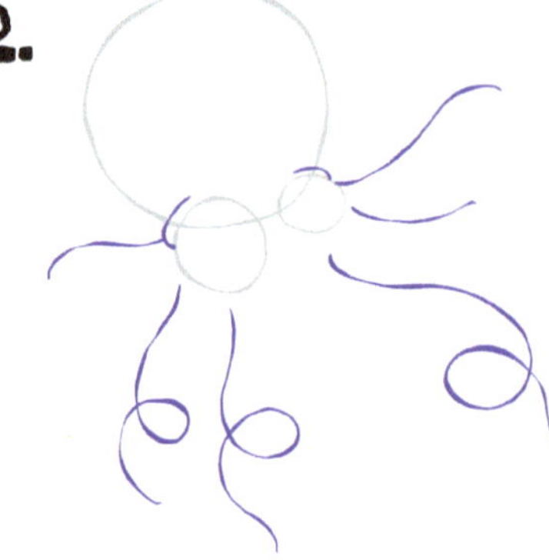

3. 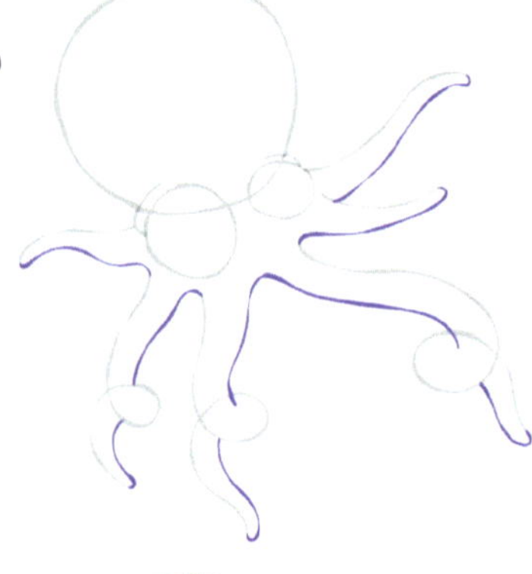

4. 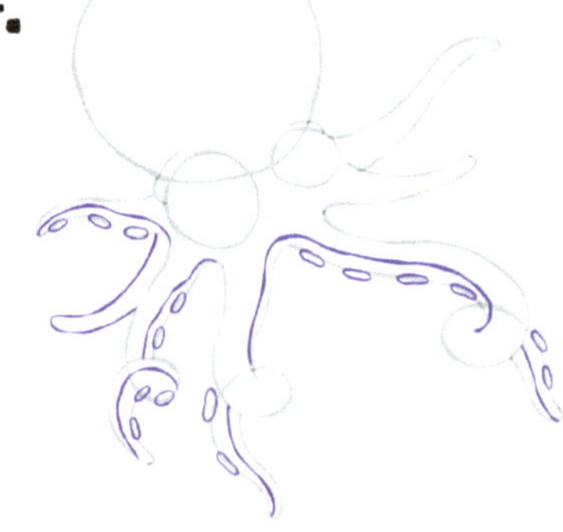

5. 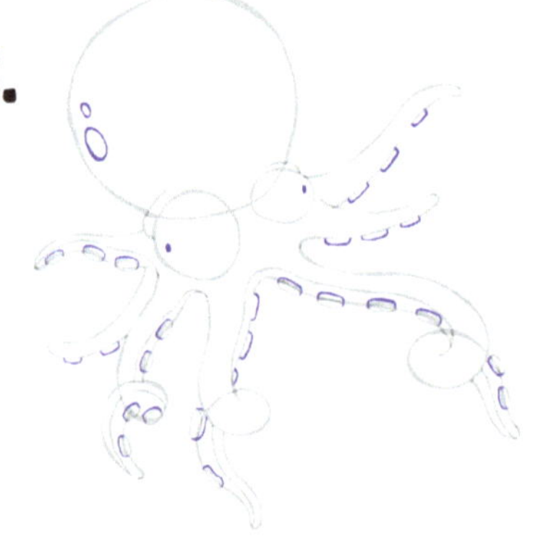

6. 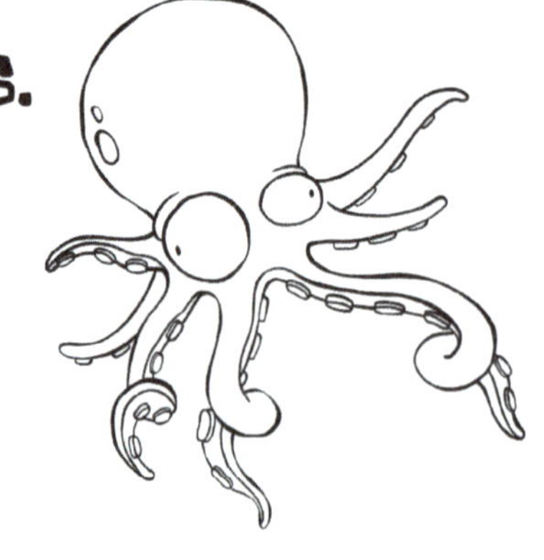

Kraken

Grim Reaper

1. 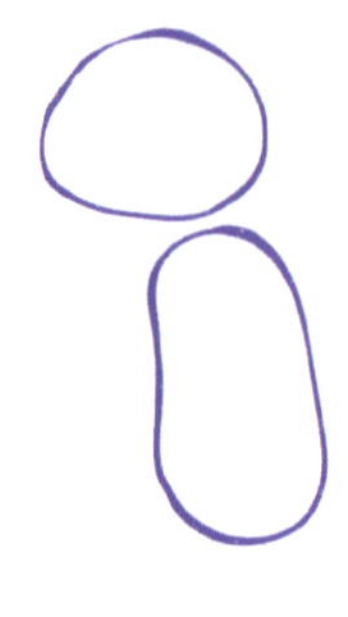

2. 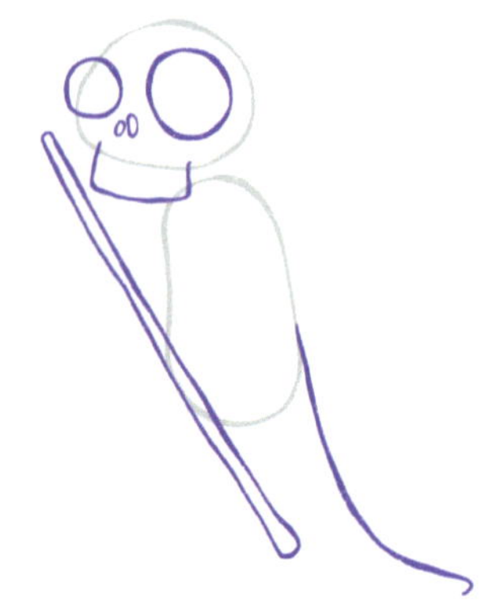

3. 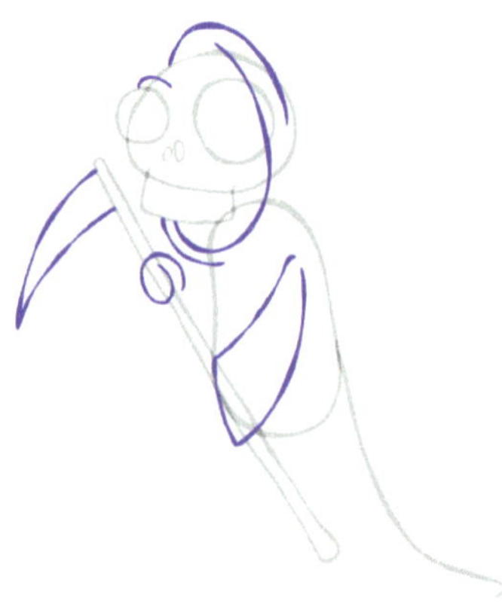

4. 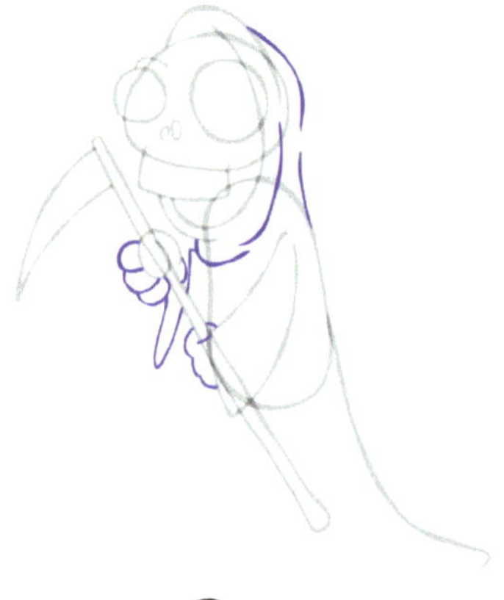

5. 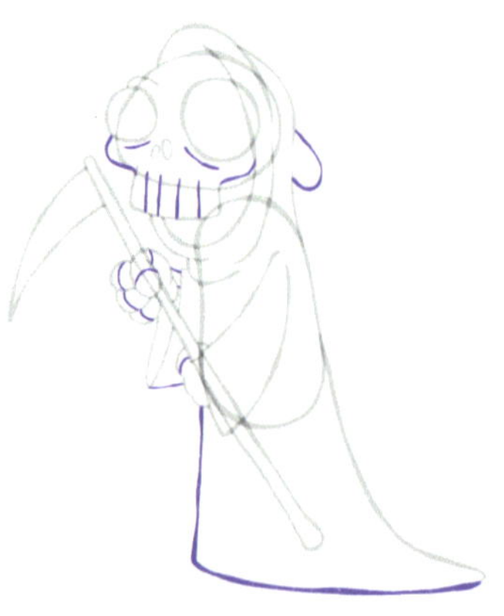

6. 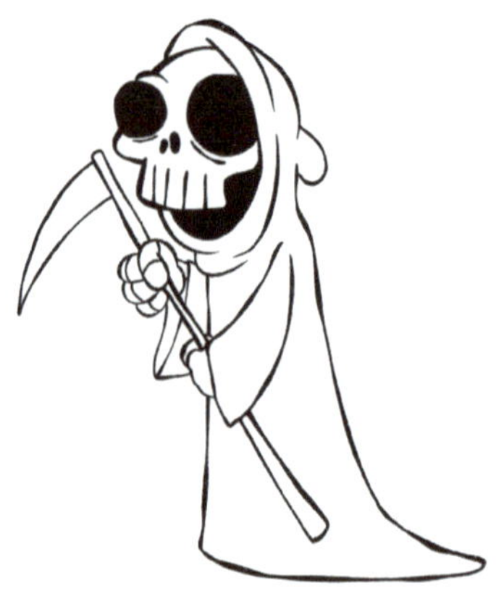

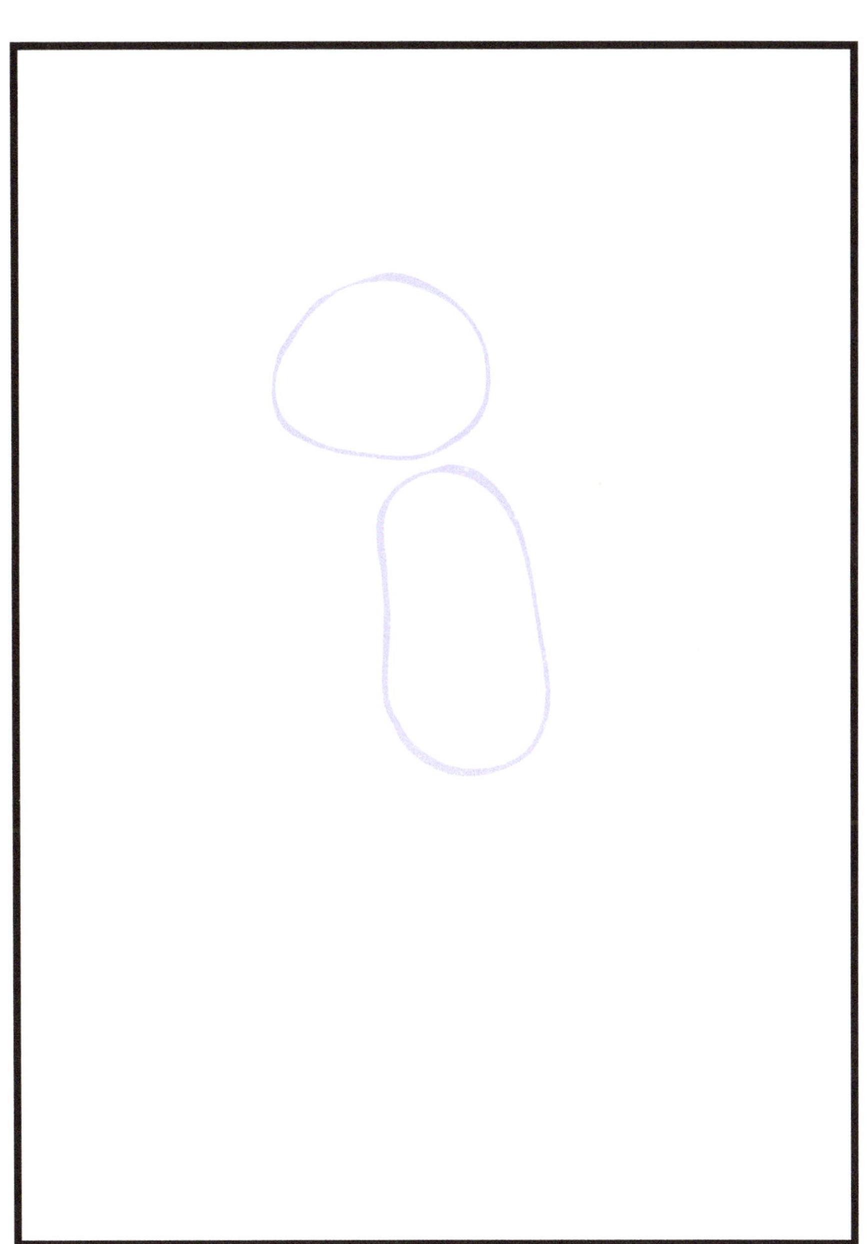
Grim Reaper - 35

Medusa

1.

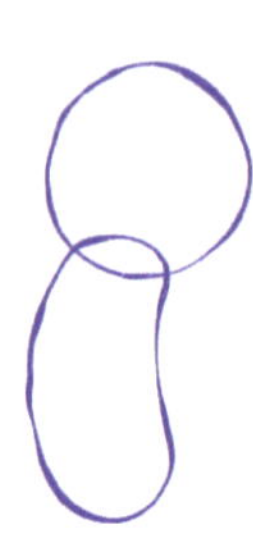

2.

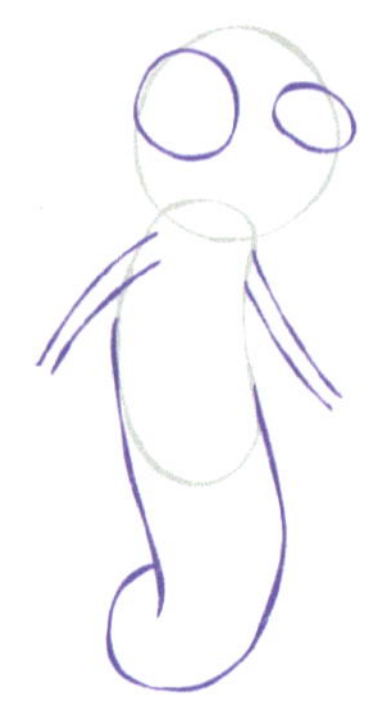

3.

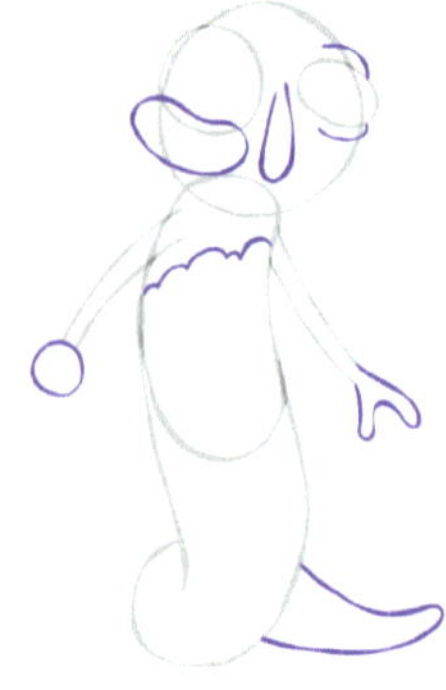

4.

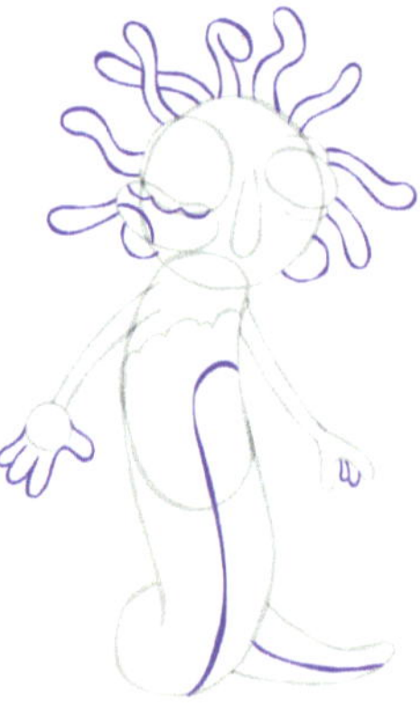

5.

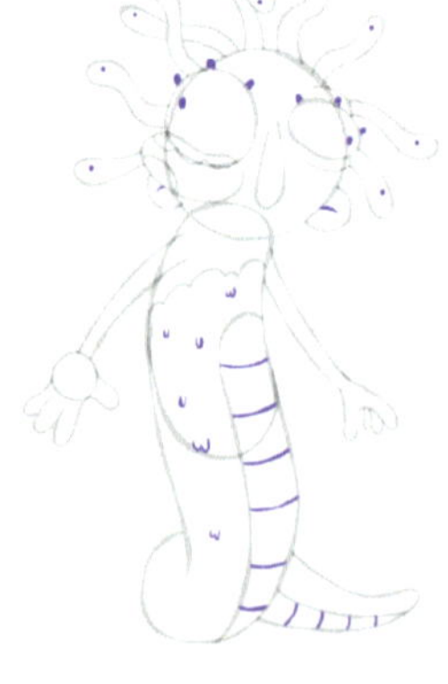

6.

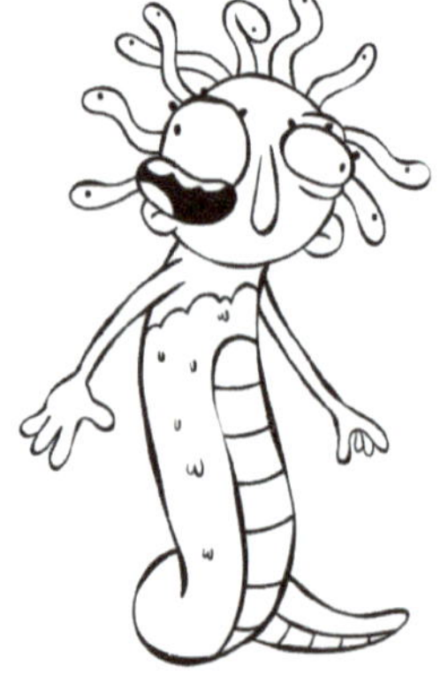

Medusa

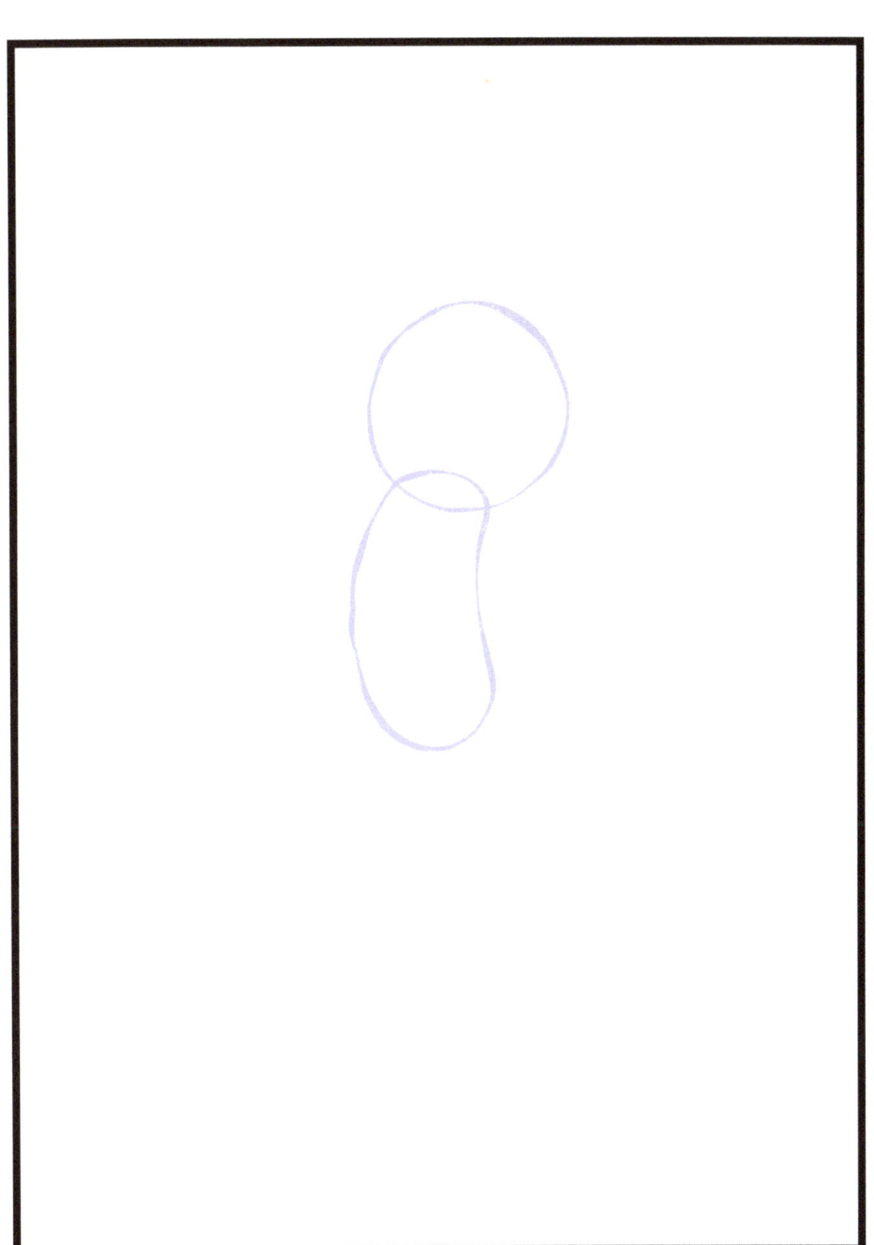

Yeti

1.

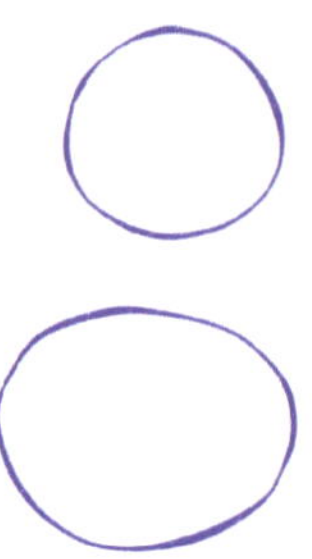

2.

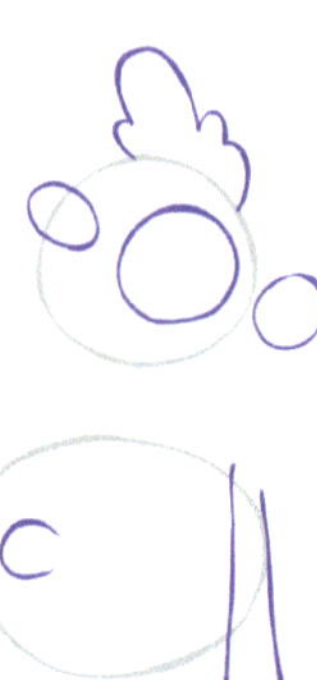

3.

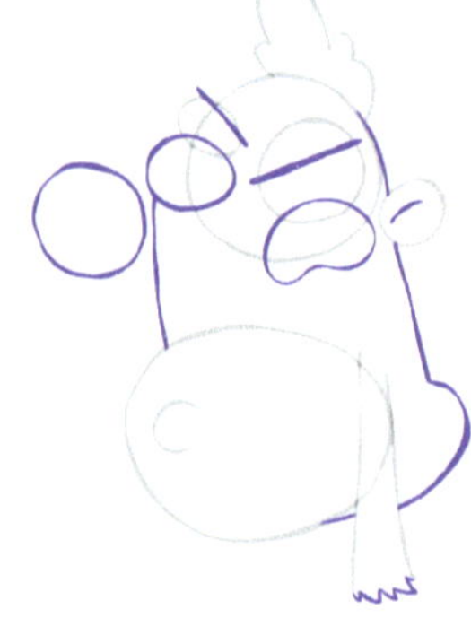

4.

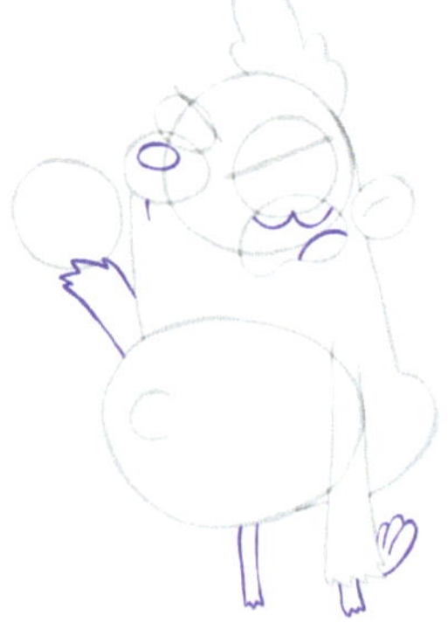

5.

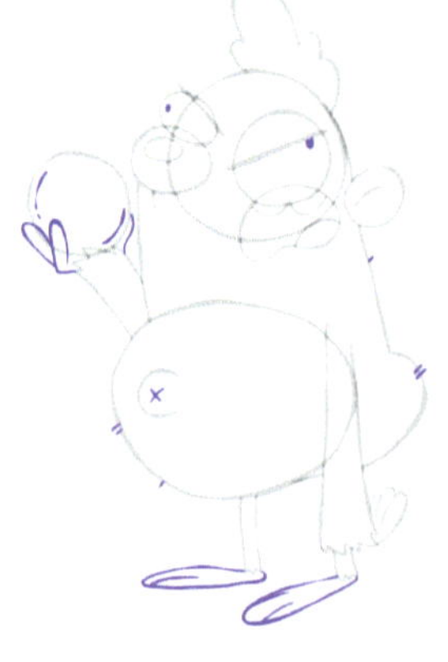

6.

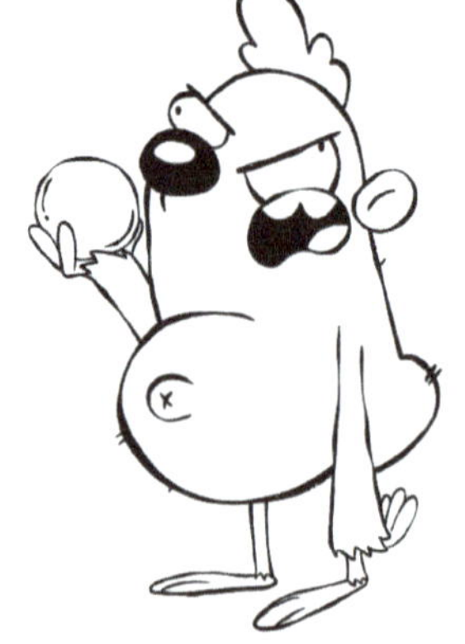

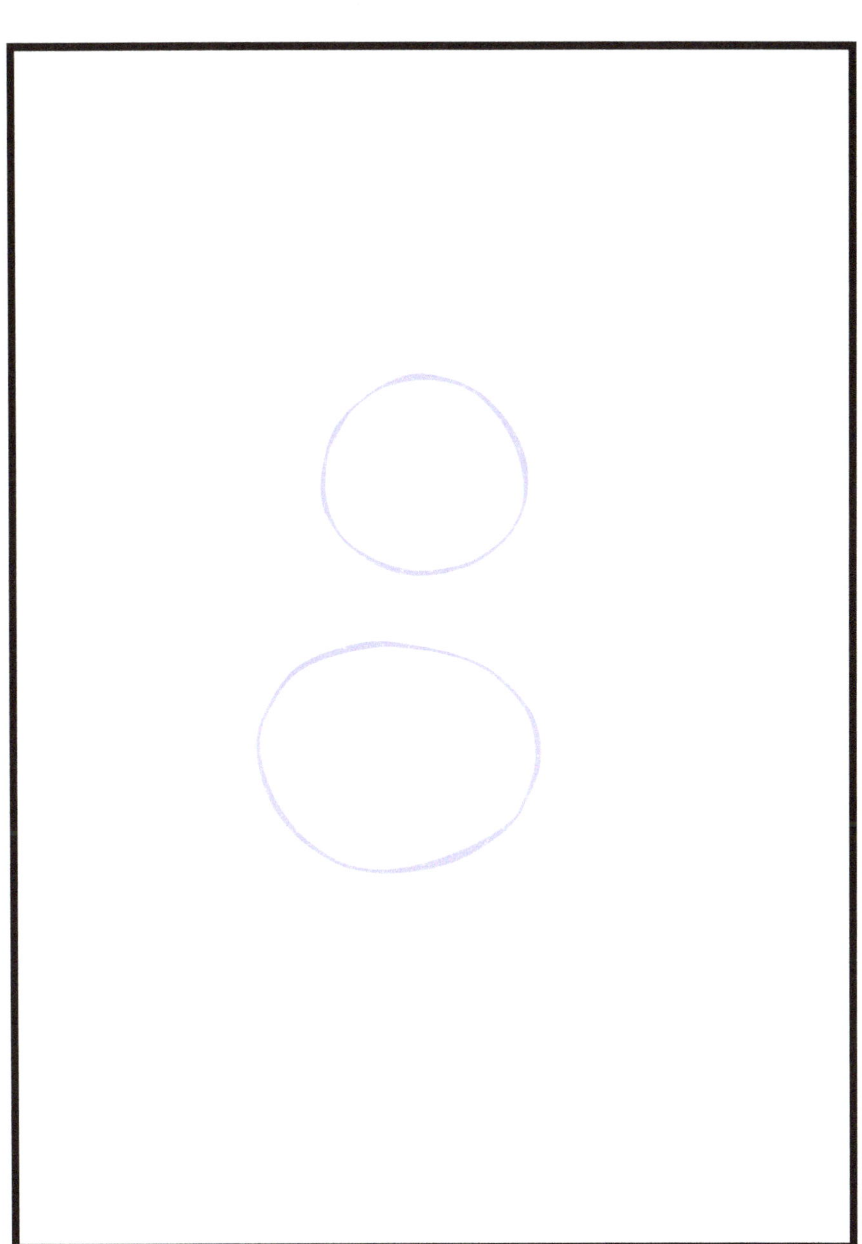

Minotaur

1.

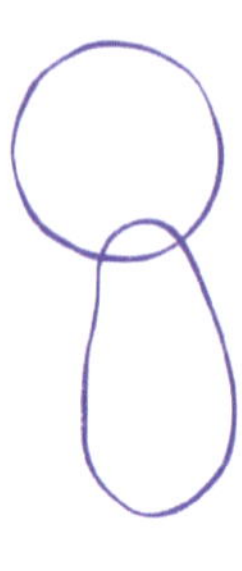

2.

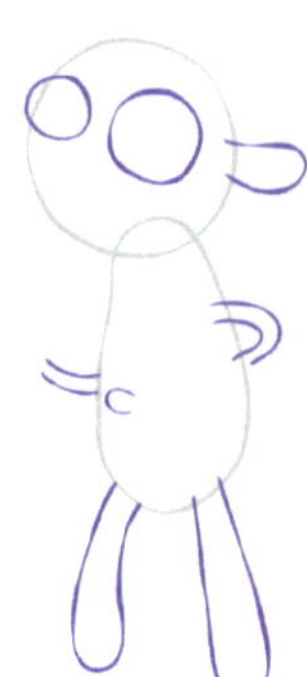

3.

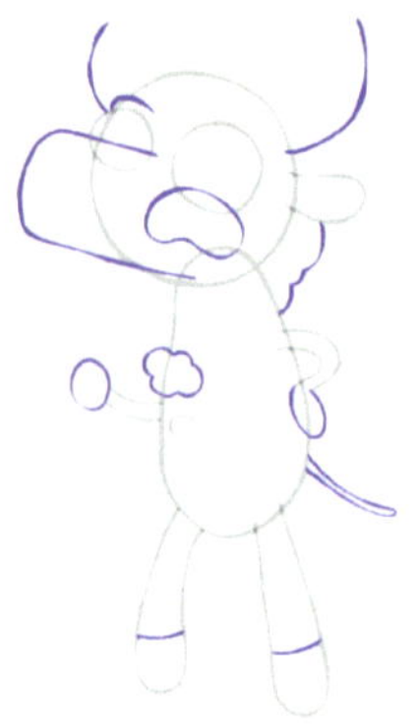

4.

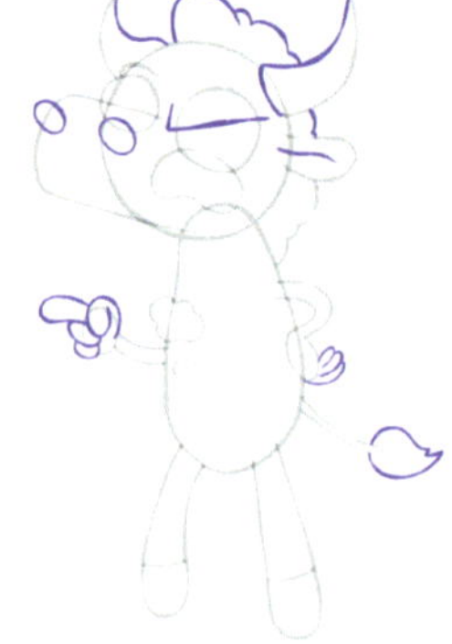

5.

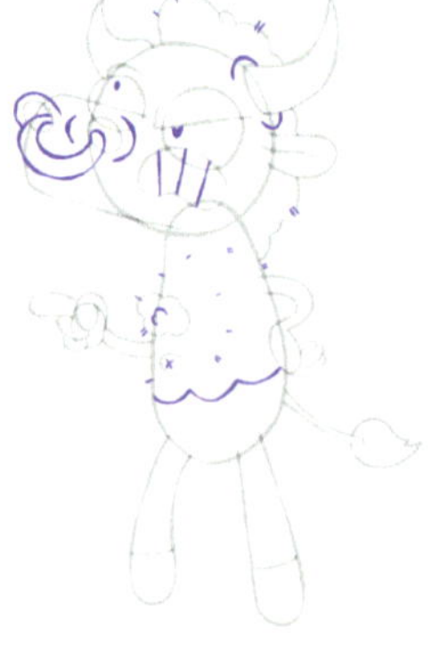

6.

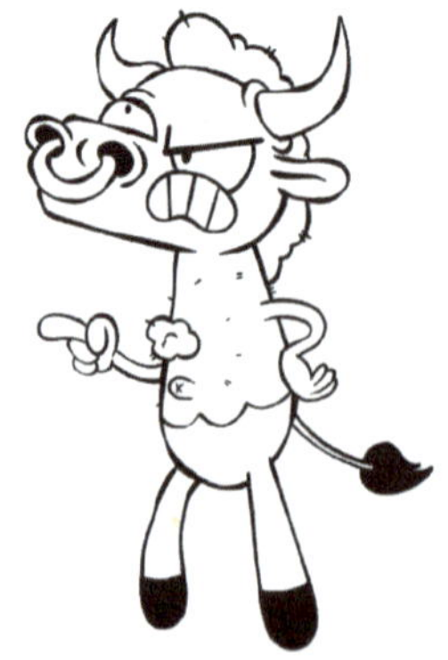

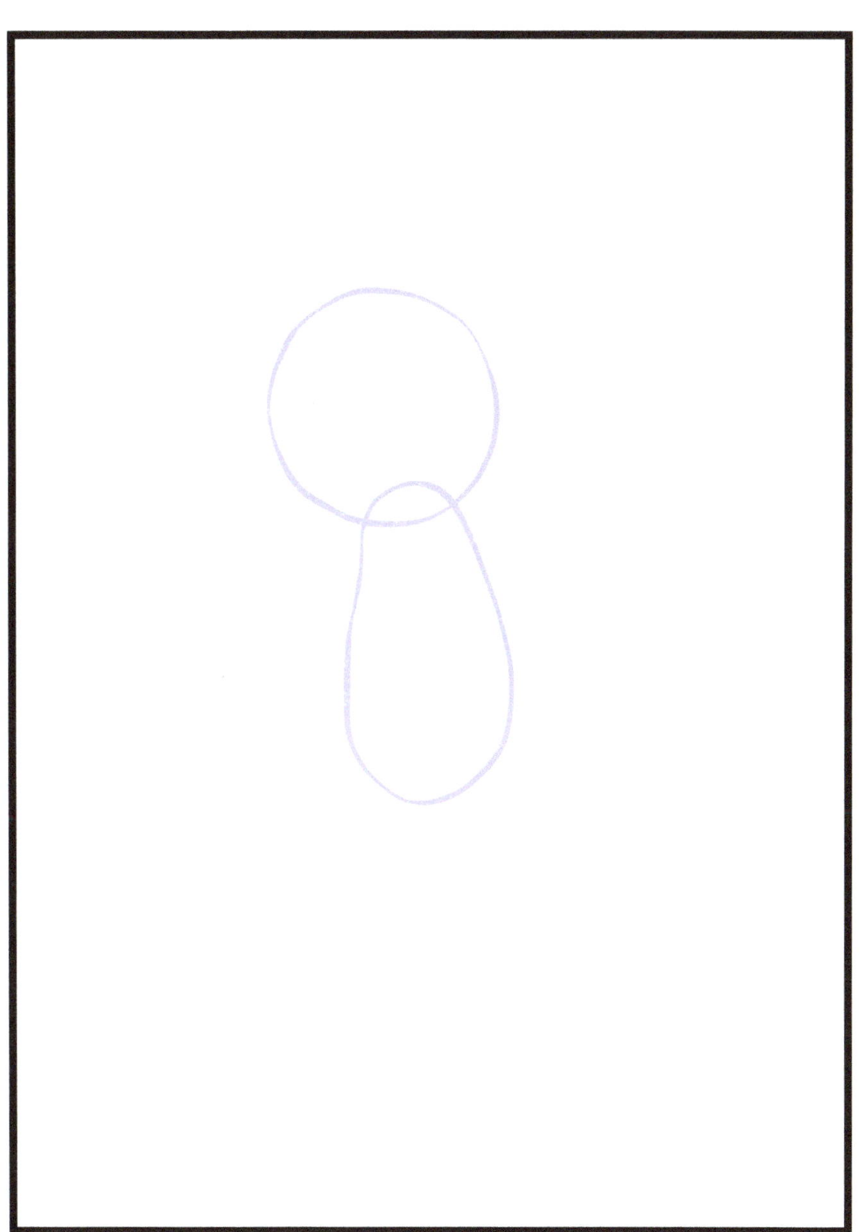

Gargoyle

1.

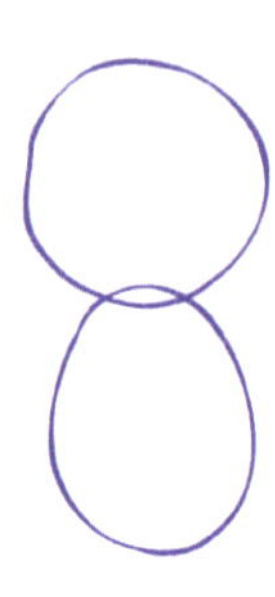

2.

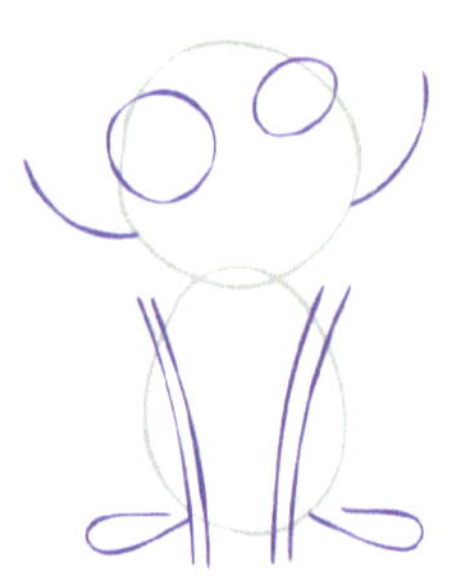

3.

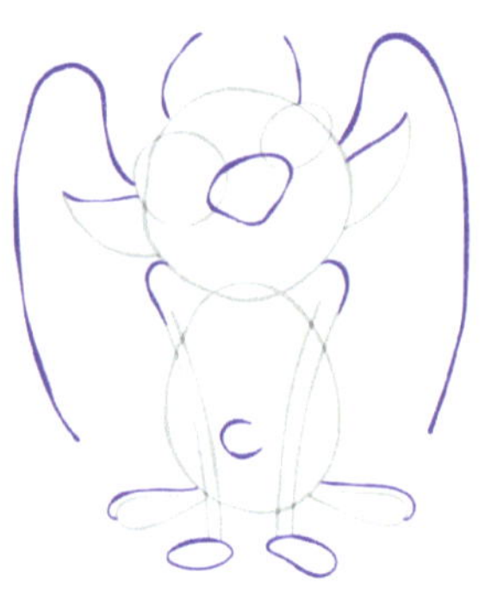

4.

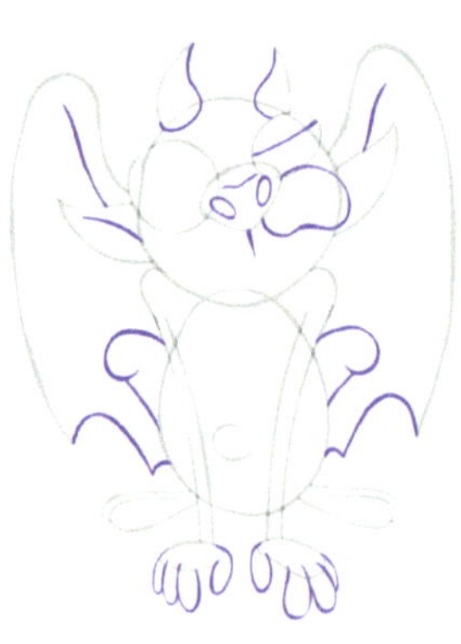

5.

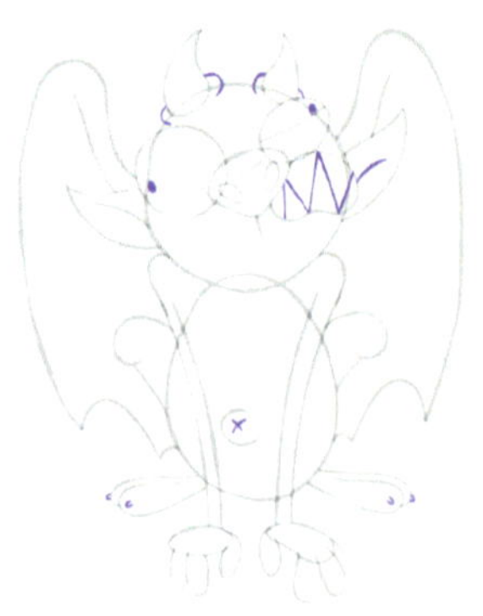

6.

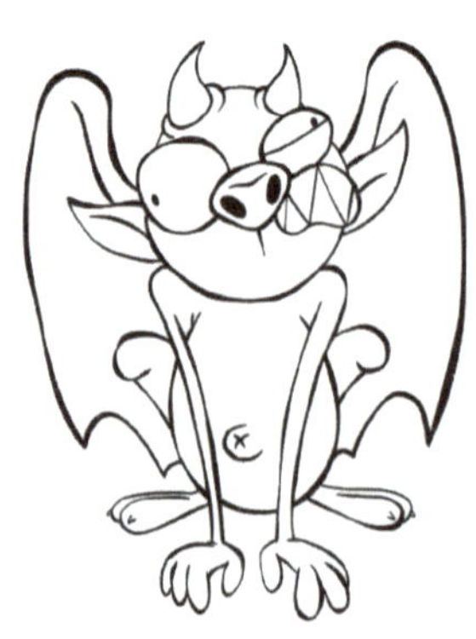

Gargoyle

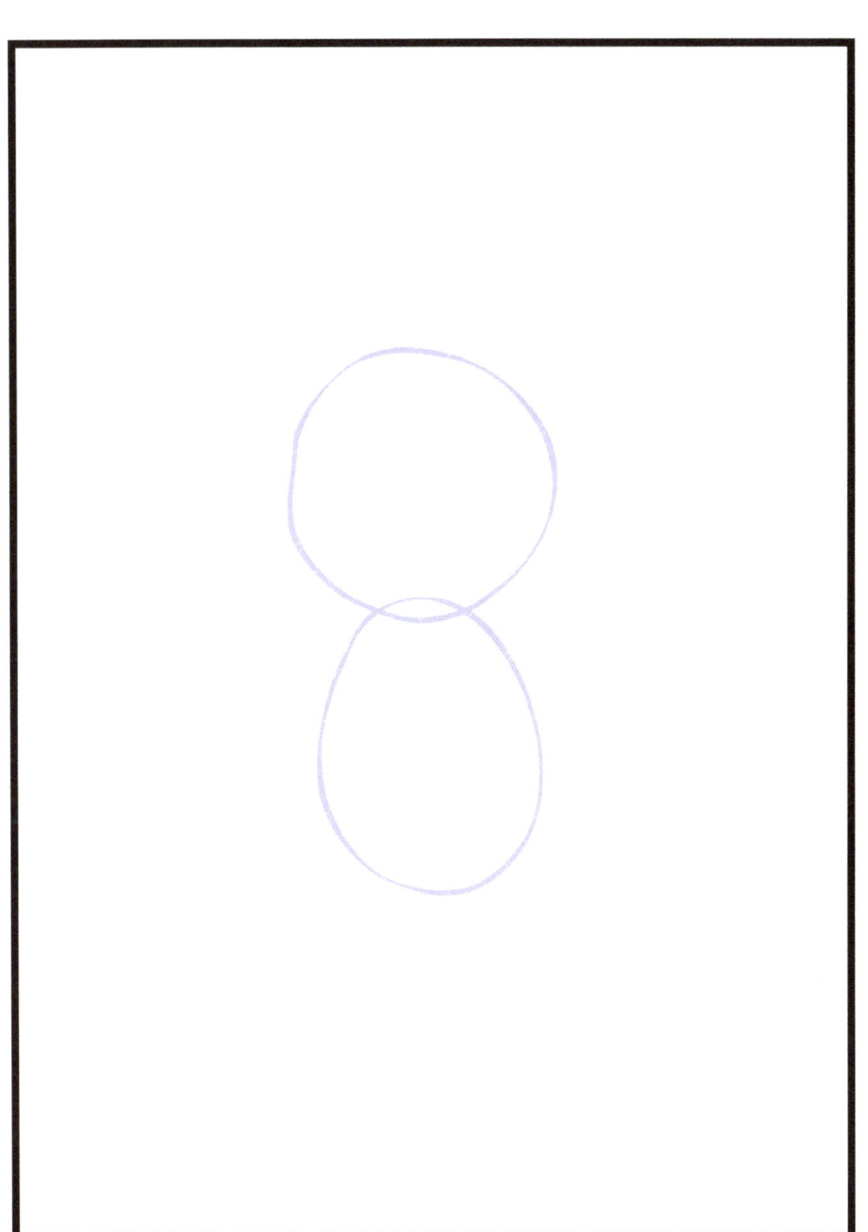

Pond Monster

1.
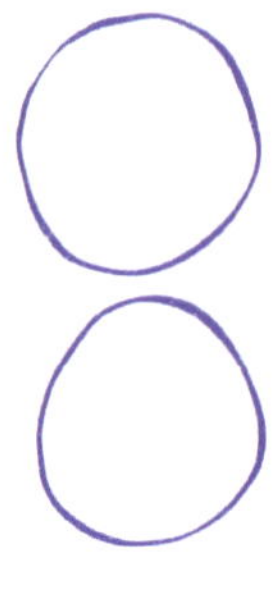

2.
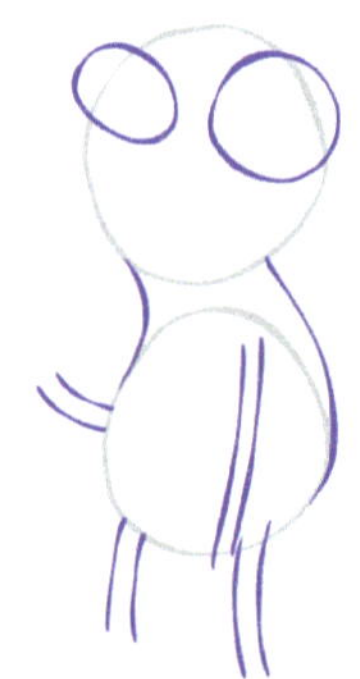

3.
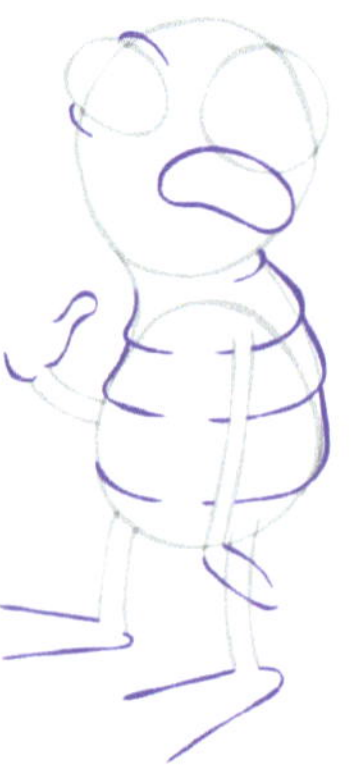

4.
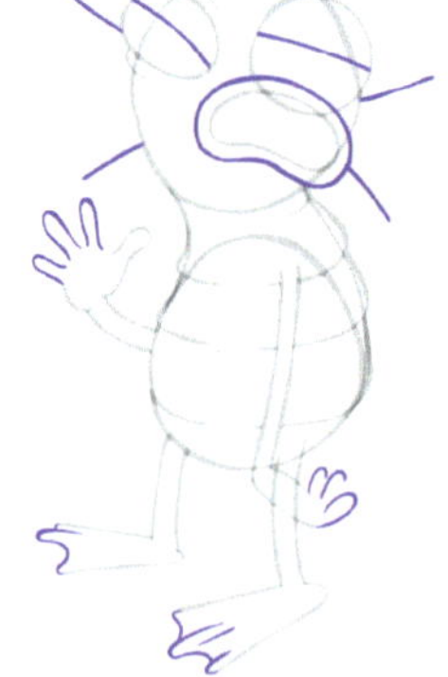

5.
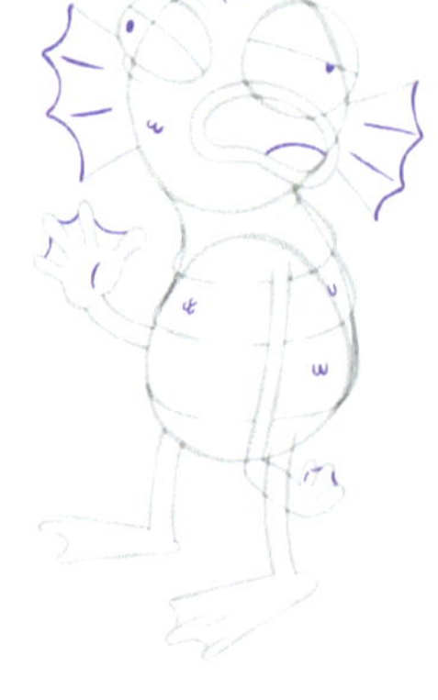

6.
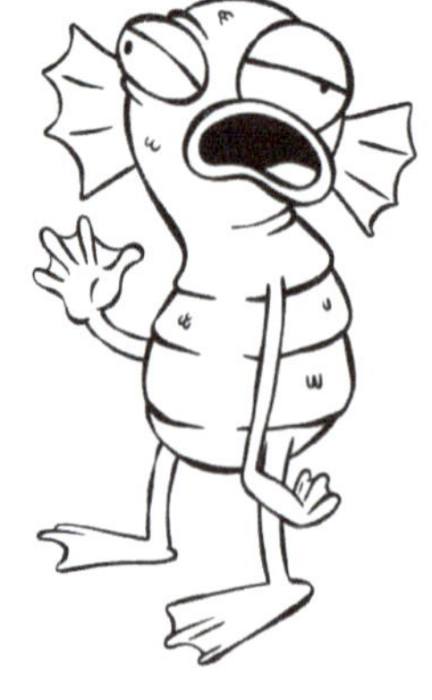

Pond Monster

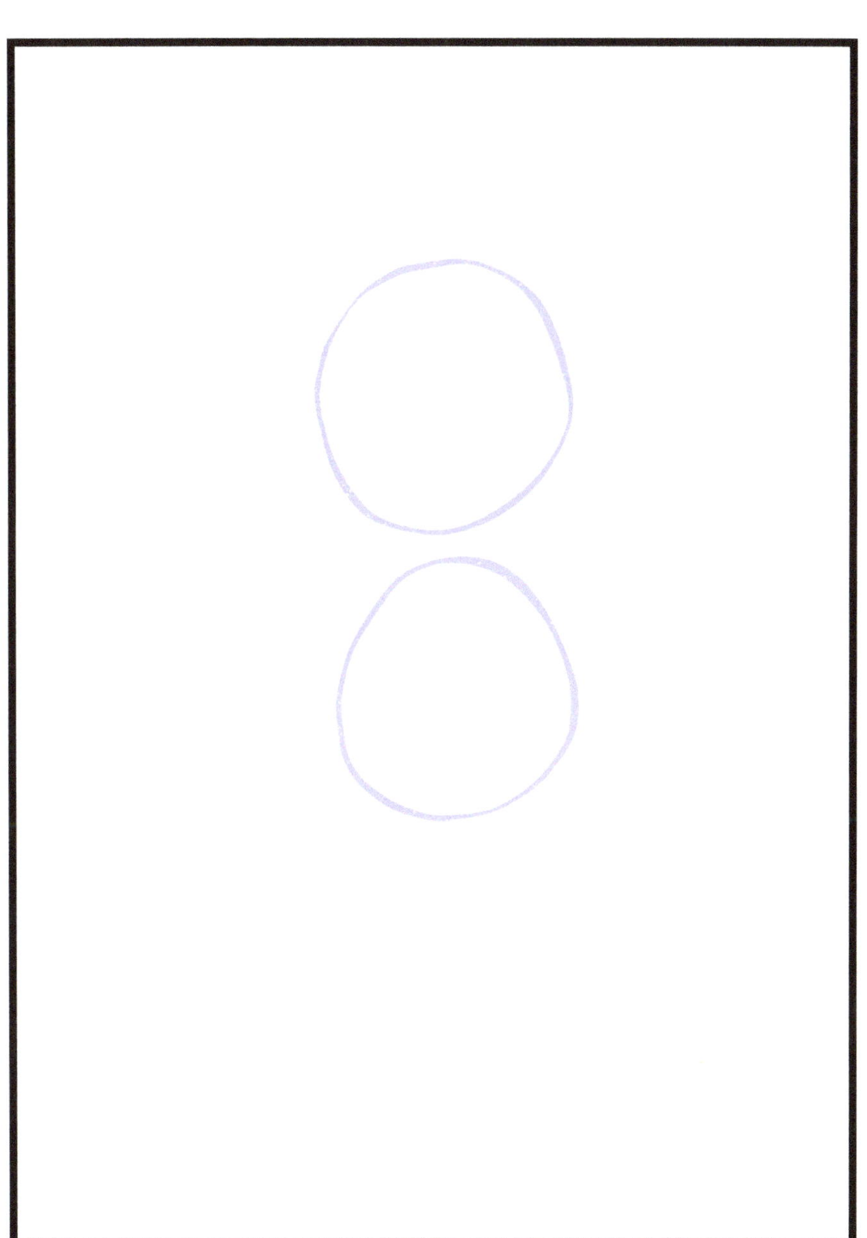

Hydra

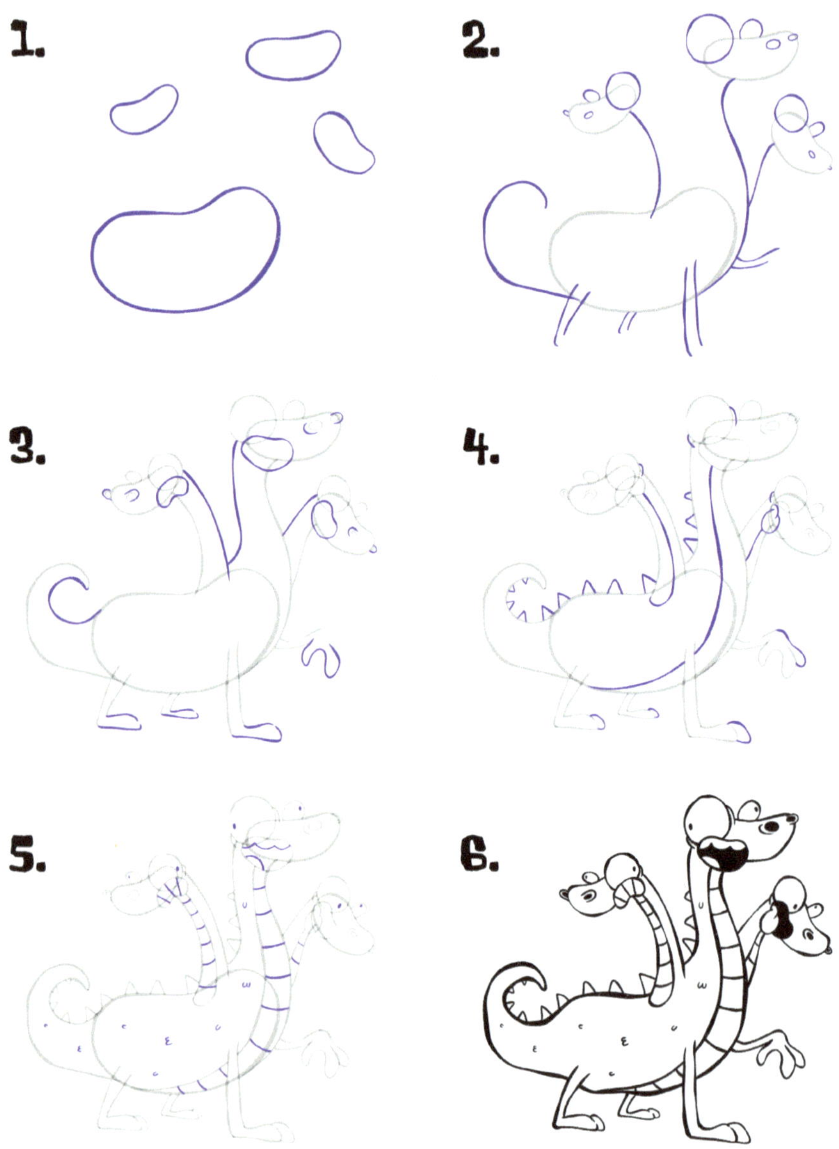

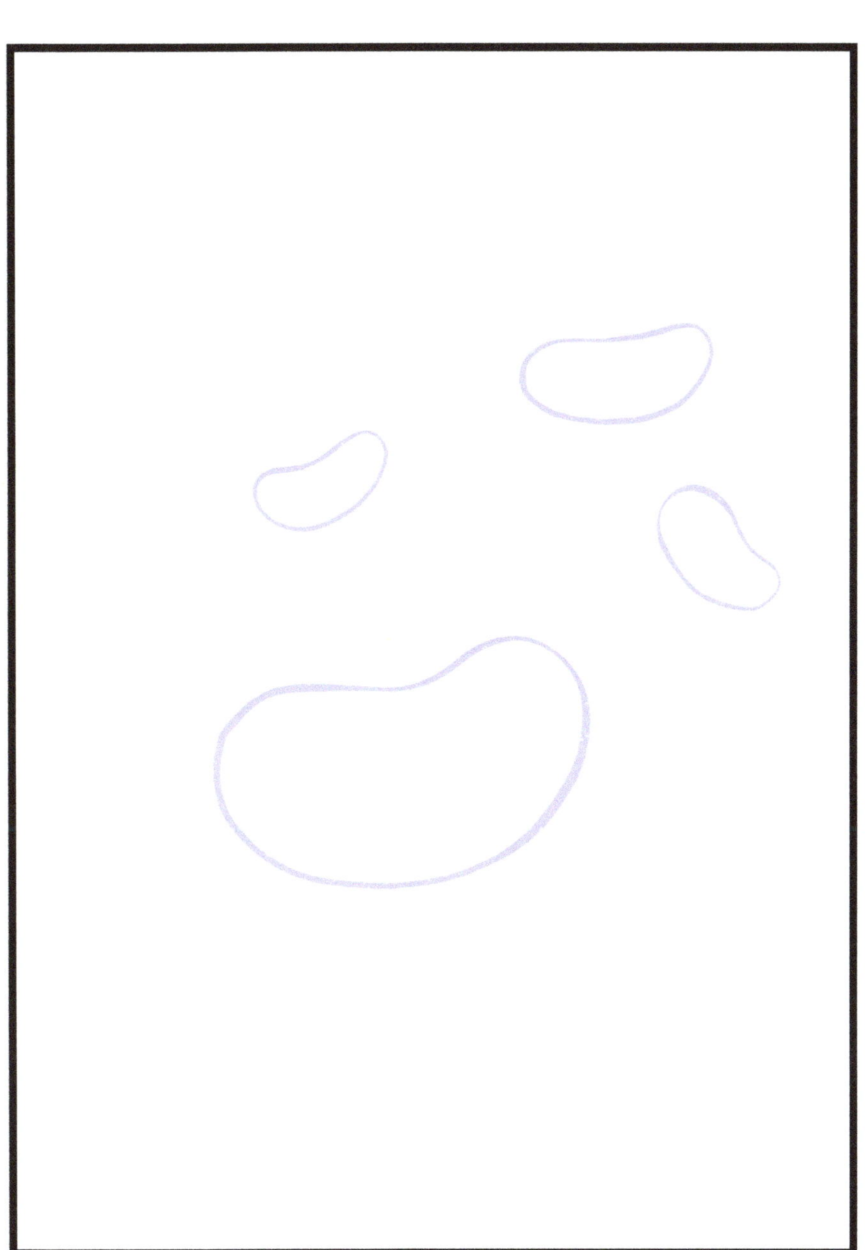

Chupacabra

1.

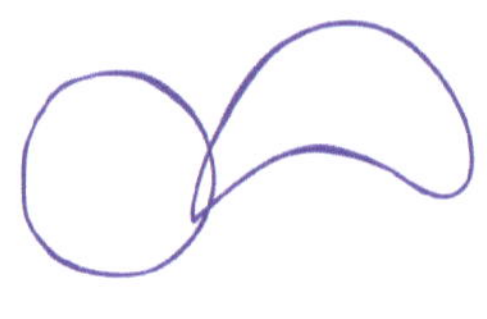

2.

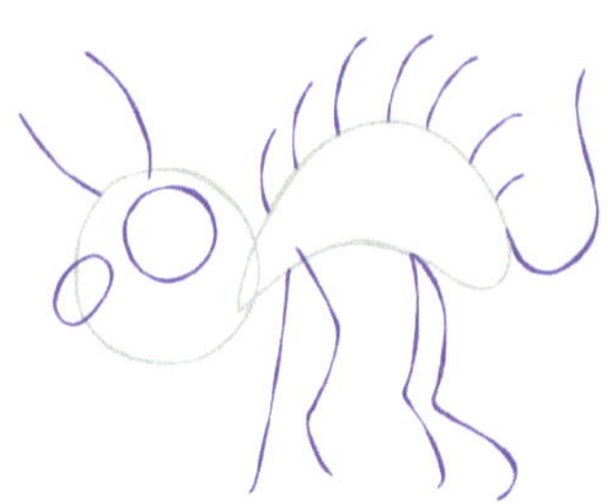

3.

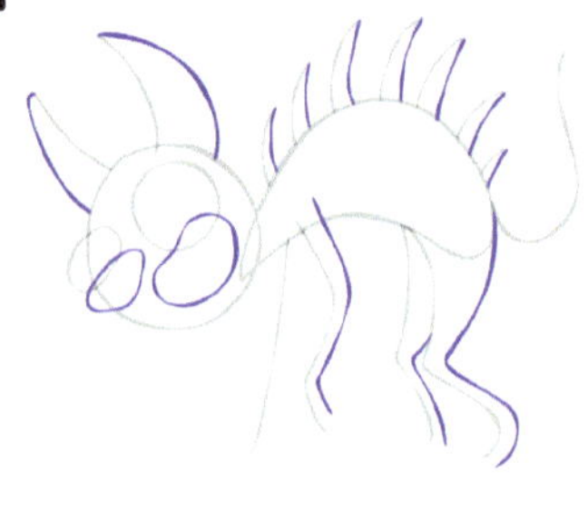

4.

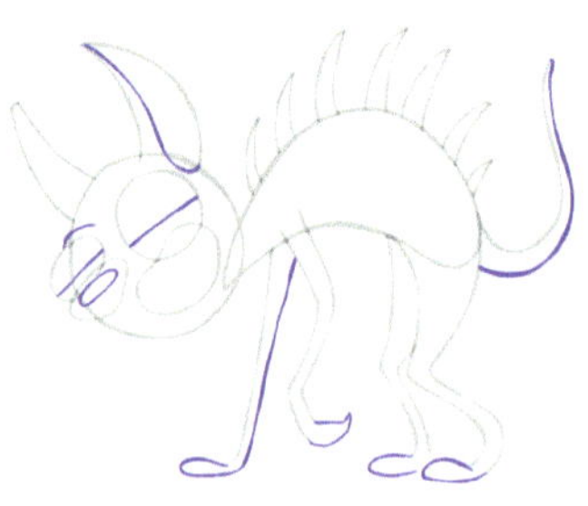

5.

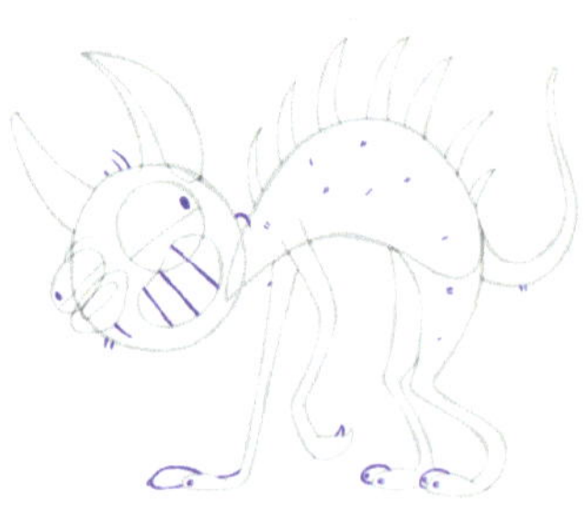

6.

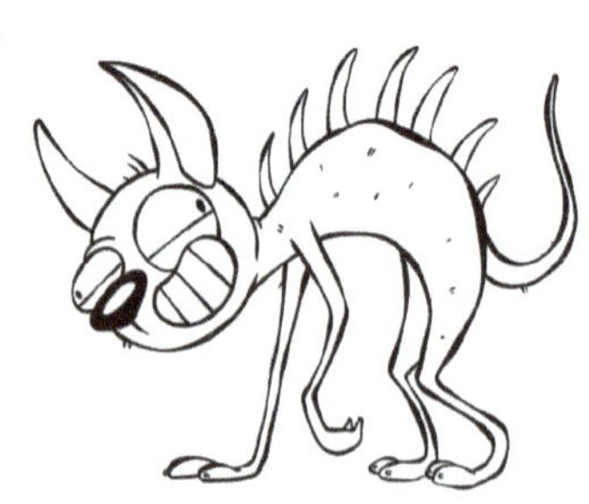

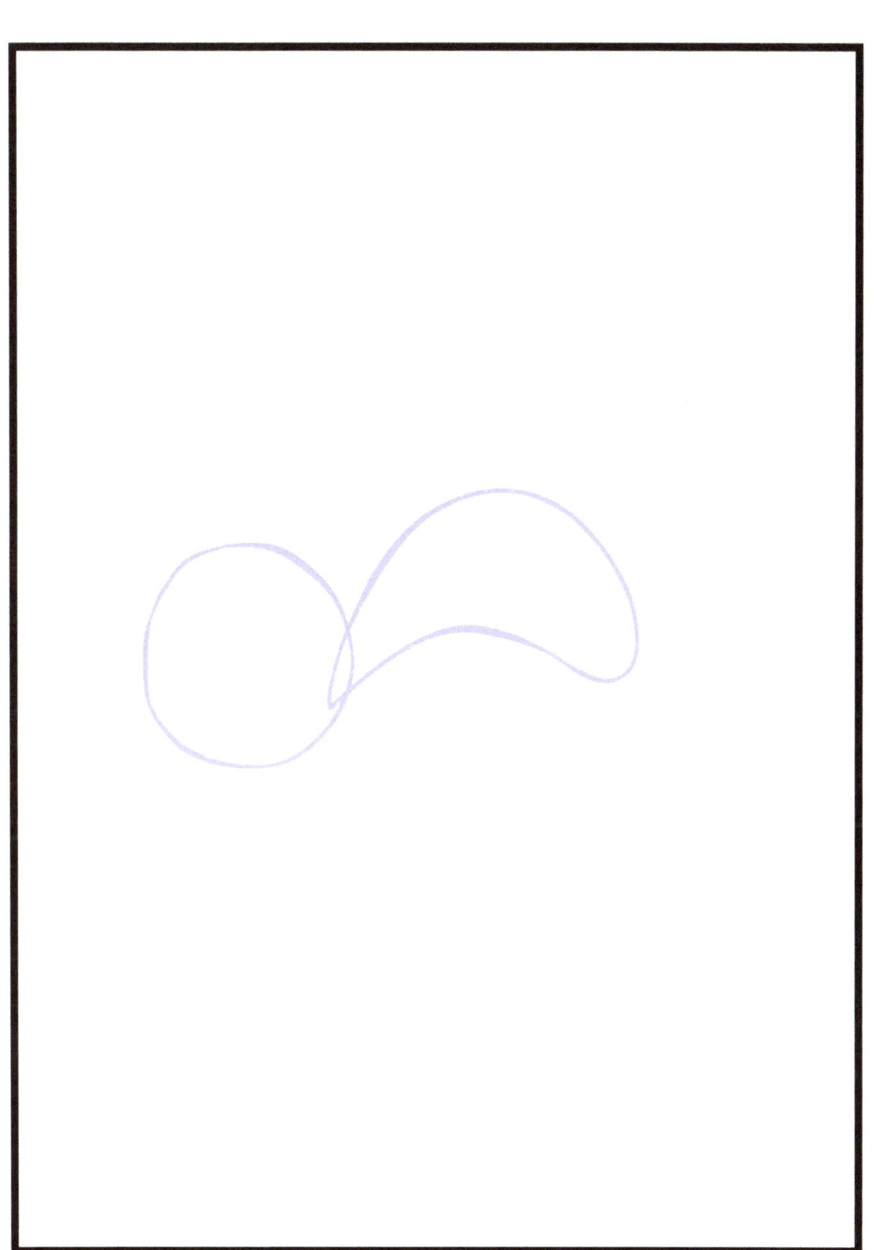

Goblin

1. 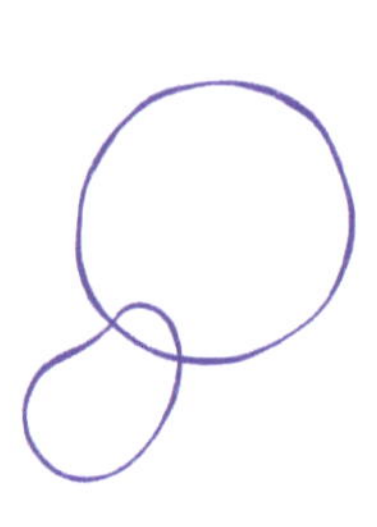

2. 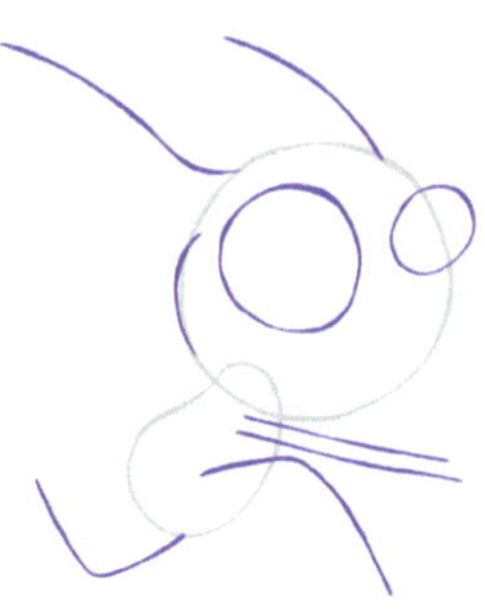

3. 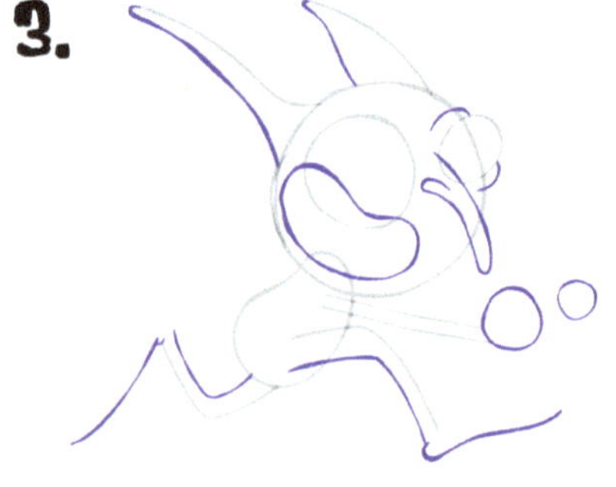

4. 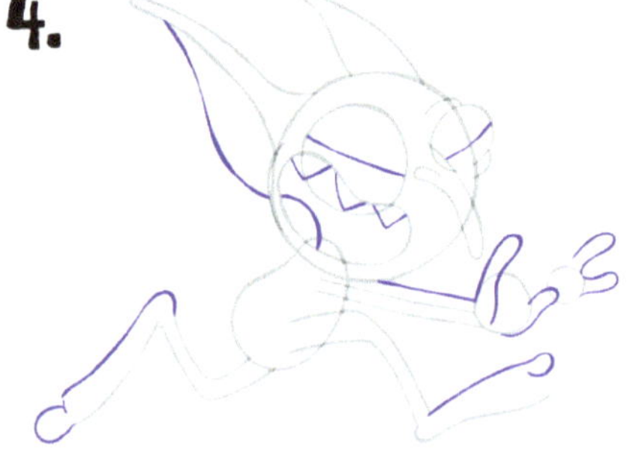

5. 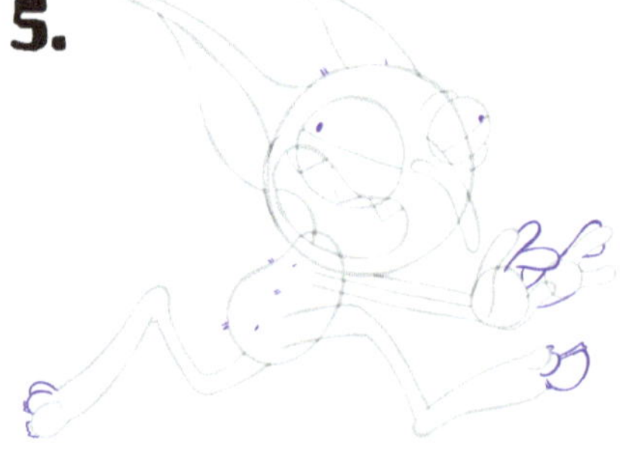

6. 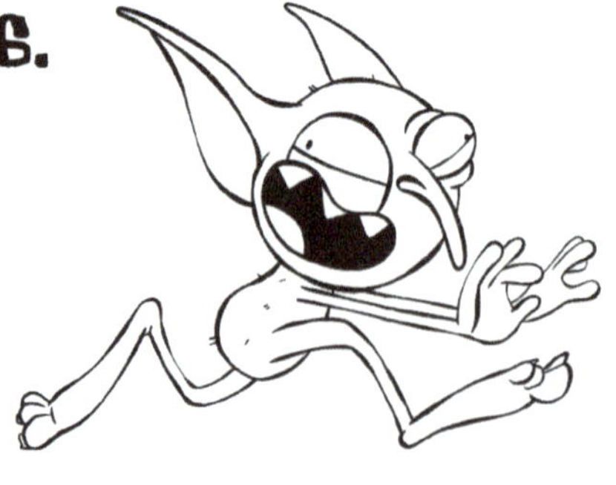

50 – Goblin

Goblin

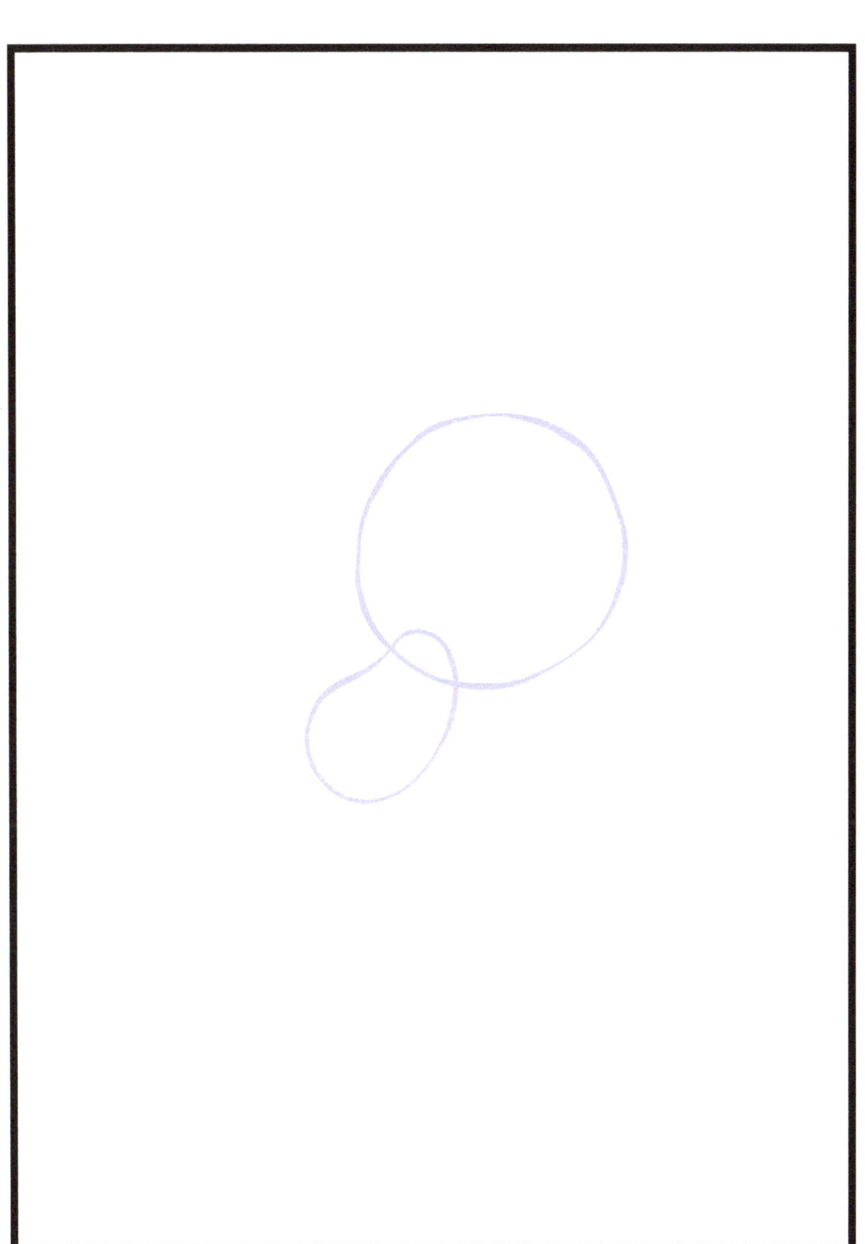

Harpy

1.

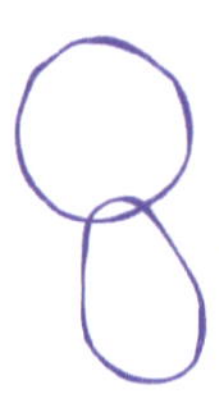

2.

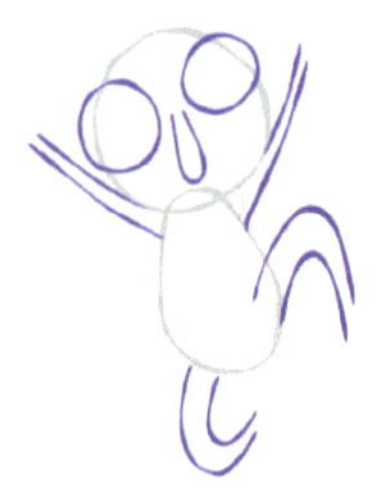

3.

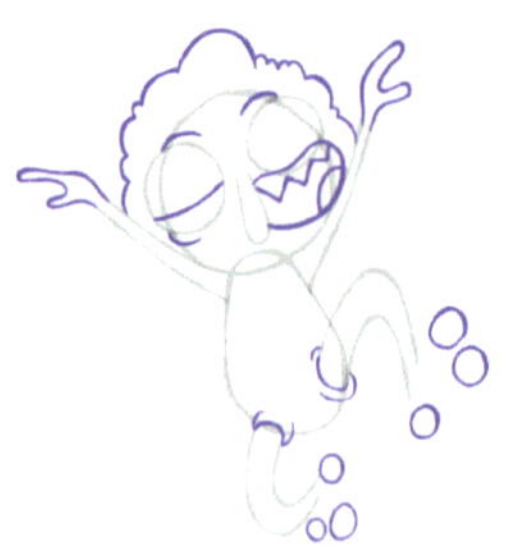

4.

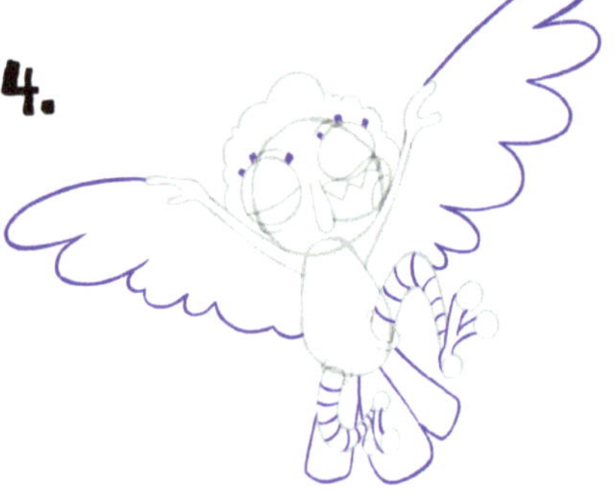

5.

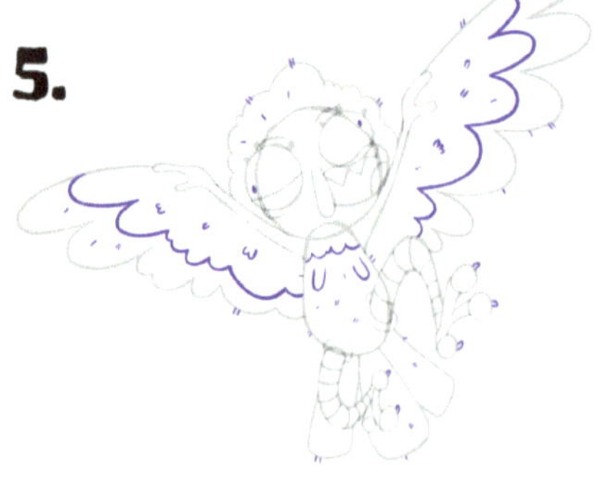

6.

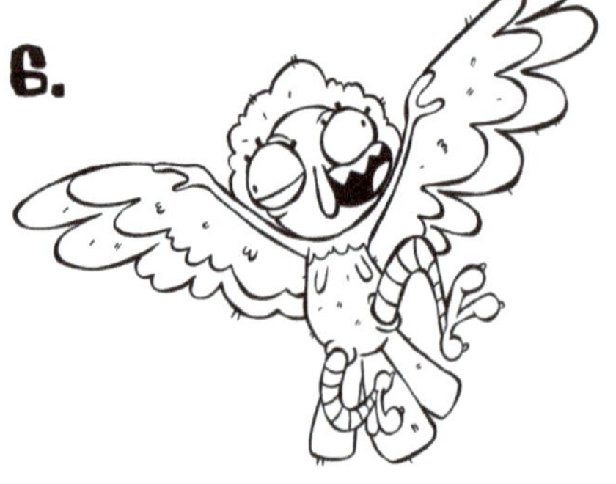

Harpy

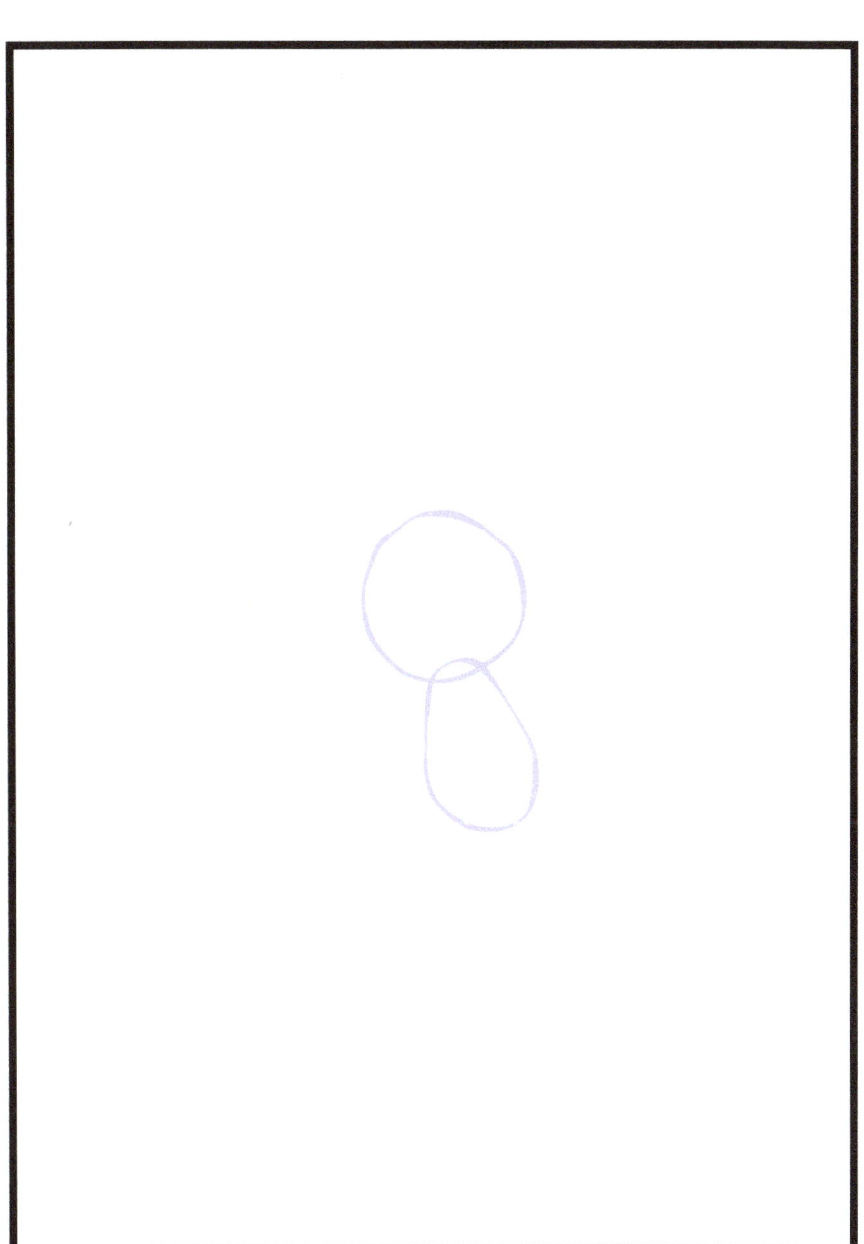

Wendigo

1.
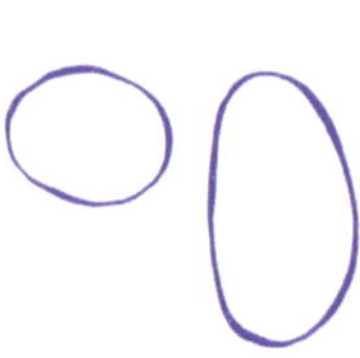

2.
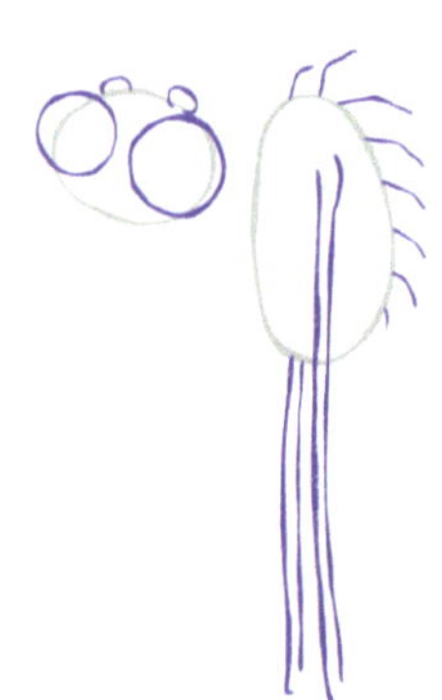

3.
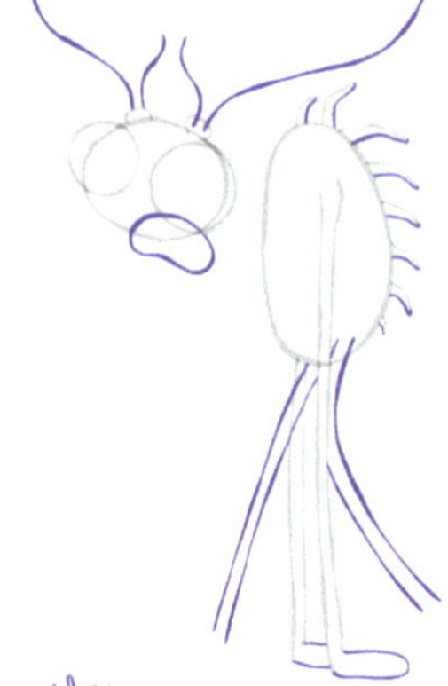

4.
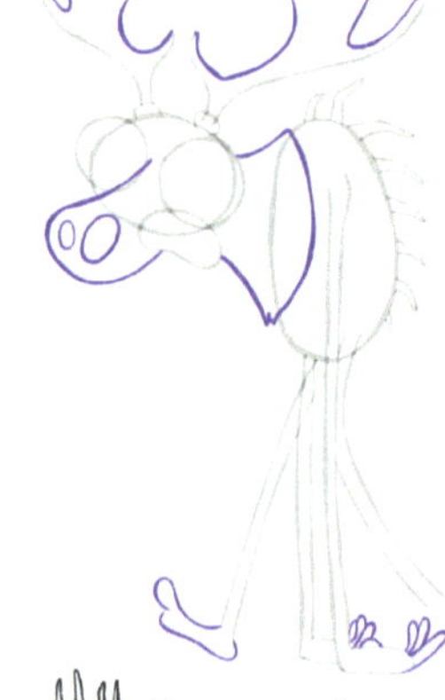

5.
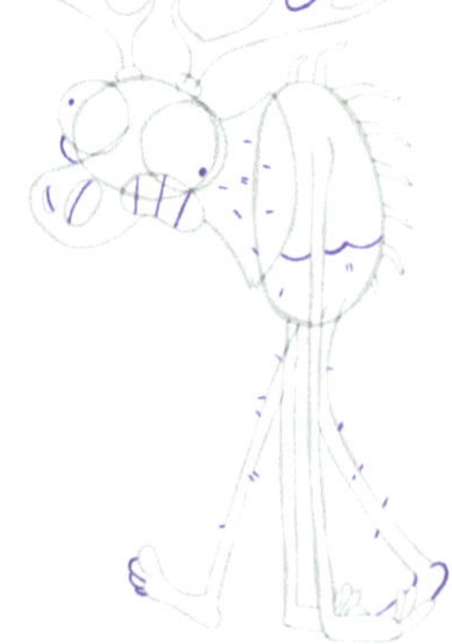

6.
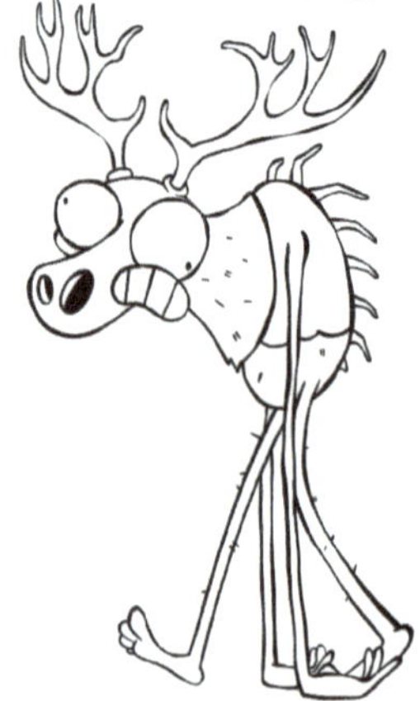

Wendigo